NEW DAYS
OLD DEMONS

Mark Driscoll

NEW DAYS
OLD DEMONS

A study of Elijah,
Sex,
Gender,
Ancient Paganism Masquerading
as Progressive Christianity,
Victims of Nothing,
Woke Politics,
the Transgender Jezebel Spirit
that Castrates Men,
and the Passive Ahab Soft
Woke Christian Beta-male Spirit
Leading the Conga Line to Sheol
Carrying a Rainbow Flag

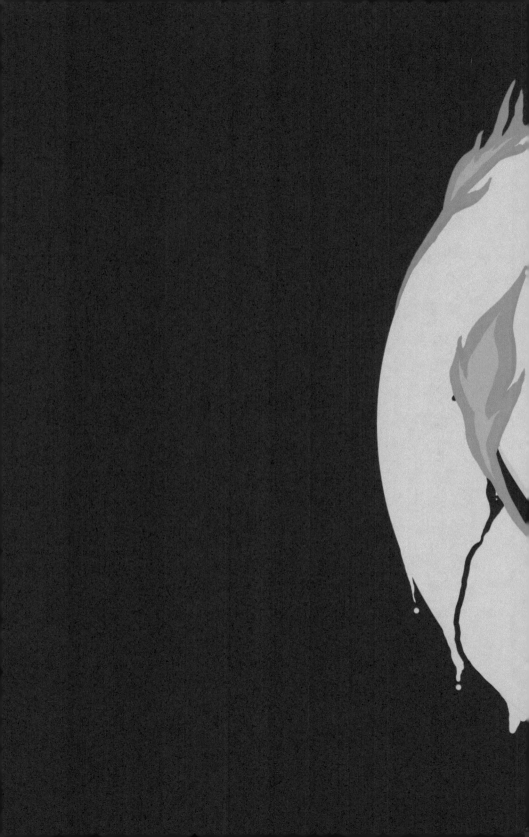

ISBN (hardcover): 979-8-9877121-8-4
ISBN (paperback): 979-8-9877121-9-1
ISBN (e-book): 979-8-9877121-7-7

Cover design, illustrations, and layout by Albatross Book Co.

Published by:
RealFaith Ministries

Thank you every member of our family for being an Elijah.

Thank you to our church family for putting up with the drama that Ahabs and Jezebels give you for having me as your pastor.

Thank you RealFaith partners who support my ministry of troublemaking.

And, thank you for picking up this book that reads like the book of Revelation meets a death metal band in a cage fight on Halloween.

CONT

ENTS

Welcome to my accidental book on
1 KINGS 17- 2 KINGS 2

**History merely repeats itself.
It has all been done before.
Nothing under the sun is truly new.**

ECCLESIASTES 1:9 (NLT)

Welcome to my accidental book.

I did not intend to write this book.

I had been preparing to preach a sermon series on Elijah and sat down during what was supposed to be a week off after Christmas in the mountains with my wife Grace, to collect my thoughts. As I started writing, things started changing. I spent most of an entire 24-hour day doing my best impression of Rain Man meets Old Testament. It was like my mind was downloading truths—many of which I had never read, heard, or thought. I ended up down numerous rabbit holes diving into biblical and historical research, pulling together tens of thousands of hours of Bible study and teaching, books about Ahab and Jezebel I'd read, and before I knew it, I had this accidental book. I've since gone back over the manuscript, adding some bits and pieces, but most of what comprises this book was written in one stream of consciousness while I was supposed to be on Christmas vacation with my wife, Grace.

As I worked through the life of Elijah, the words of Jesus from Matthew 24:8 kept echoing in my mind, "All these are but the beginning of the birth pains." In context, Jesus is talking about the signs of the end of the age, what the world will be like as we get closer to the persecution of God's people and increase of evil before the Second Coming of Jesus Christ. In this section of Scripture, Jesus foretells the destruction of the Temple, which happened in 70 A.D., which would be followed by false christs that were counterfeit anti-Christs; the increase of political conflict and wars led by evil rulers of godless nations; and physical and natural disasters referred to as "famines" and "earthquakes". Following all of this will be the outlawing of Christian faith, tribulation, martyrdom, increasing hatred of believers, and mass apostasy as numerous people fall away from the faith. Everything Jesus prophesied occurred to a lesser degree than the last days in the days of Elijah in the nation of Israel under the demonic rule of King Ahab and Queen Jezebel.

When Jesus uses the language of "birth pains", He is saying that history will be born again just as believers are. When we were born, our mothers experienced great pain and pressure that slowly increased until the suffering was unbearable. But, out of this suffering came birth and new life. Jesus is saying that the closer we get to the end of this age and the beginning of the age to come, the birth pains will get more frequent and intense. The underlying conclusion I came to that resulted in this Bible study book is that the same demons and pains at work in Elijah's day continue in our day with greater frequency and intensity and will continue until Jesus returns and births eternity and newness of life. Preceding the Second Coming of Jesus will be the Second Coming of Elijah, something we will study near the end of this book. Behind the birth pains are often demonic forces at work in and through political and spiritual leaders causing spiritual warfare in the seen and unseen realms. This fact explains why we see the same birth pains in various times and places, caused by various leaders because, although we are living in new days, we are dealing with old demons, which is the theme of our deep dive Bible study into the lives of Elijah, Ahab, Jezebel, and Jesus Christ.

National Geographic has reported that there is a significant increase in the worship of ancient pagan demon gods saying, "Centuries ago, ancient Celts traveled windy moors to worship the horned god, Cernunnos. Ancient Egyptians crossed deserts to invoke the protection of Isis. Druids journeyed to a forest clearing to perform rituals under the moon. But over time, such deities faded into myth; the rituals went underground. Recently, however, a resurgence of interest in Pagan practices—crystals and tarot cards, astrology, and herbal magic—has brought Paganism from the fringes back to the center of pop culture, or at least to the top of your TikTok feed. At least 1.5 million people in the United States identify as Pagans—up from 134,000 in 2001. They range from Wiccans and Kemetics to TikTok witches and heathens." There is, in general, a move away from organized religions and toward spirituality," says Helen Berger, an author and sociologist of contemporary Paganism and witchcraft. Female empowerment and gay rights movements, the climate crisis, and a desire for a more life-affirming religion have fueled interest in the growing spiritual community, she adds" ... "It's very difficult to sum up what Paganism 'is' since there is so much diversity," says Sarah Pike, author and professor of comparative religion at California State University, Chico. "Pagans view the natural world as sacred. They celebrate the interconnectedness of all things, seeing humans, nature, and spiritual beings as part of a web of life" ... After centuries of persecution, Paganism remained mainly a fringe practice until the 1960s. It became an attractive religion to follow for those rebelling against restrictive social norms. In the past decade, the rise of TikTok—#witchtok has more than 35 billion views—and popular TV shows like the *Chilling Adventures of Sabrina, Vikings, Supernatural,* and *American Horror Story: Coven* are helping drive increased interest in the spiritual movement."[a]

The demonic and paganism are making a comeback to the center of western life and culture. The old demons are back in new days doing what they've always done—lead people astray.

As we delve into the life and ministry of Elijah, a few principles are helpful to keep in mind.

One, the Bible is not old, but rather eternal. When something is old, it becomes outdated and irrelevant. The Bible is timeless, which means that it is always timely and never gets old.

Two, the Bible does not tell us what happened, but what always happens. As we examine the themes and principles of the life and ministry of Elijah, we see God versus government, passive men, controlling women, sexual seduction, lying through powerful false prophets, woke syncretistic churches, and cancelled truth-telling prophets, which is all still happening in our day.

Three, we need to look both at the story of Elijah in the past and look through the story of Elijah to understand the present and future. Because Elijah is a prophet with a prophetic ministry, his life, teaching, and experiences were intended to serve as a worldview lens through which we interpret and understand the cultural context of ministry today and tomorrow. As Romans 15:4 says, "whatever was written in former days was written for our instruction, that through endurance and through the encouragement of the Scriptures we might have hope."

Four, even though we are living in new days, we are dealing with old demons. When we see eerily similar trends in politics, culture, gender, sexuality, and spirituality in completely different time periods, nations, and cultures being led through different human beings, we must ask if it's a recurring coincidence, or the same demon working in different eras through different people? Camille Paglia is a rather honest lesbian atheistic American feminist academic known for her cultural critique and support of the biological basis of one's sexual identity. Not a fan of Christianity and an advocate of decriminalizing everything from abortion to drugs, and pornography, she does share some very interesting observations in her two-volume analysis of Western culture and art called *Sexual Personae: Art and Decadence from Nefertiti to Emily Dickinson* and *Sex, Art, and American Culture*. She examines the pagan symbolism omnipresent in Western art, and the unity and continuity of western culture in both volumes. In the first volume, Paglia talks about "ghosts", and the "daemonic" as neutral spirits, which Christians, she said, refer to as the demonic and evil diving beings. She seeks to prove that Christianity did not defeat paganism in the West, but instead paganism survived and thrived in sex, art, and "carnal red media" in which "Our eyes and ears are drowned in a sensual torrent". She goes on to say that this cultural paganism with its'"daemonic vitality" is the Church's greatest threat in our day. Why? Because "paganism is eye intense". Furthermore, "The war between Judeo-Christianity and paganism is still being waged in the latest ideologies of the university." In the second volume, Paglia shows how there have been similar historical figures throughout Western culture. For example, she compares Venus and Medusa with Marilyn Monroe and Madonna. She also compares Elizabeth Taylor to Cleopatra, calling her "Hollywood's pagan queen". As an atheist, Paglia does not seriously consider that new days have old demons doing the same old thing through new people, but in this book we will.

Five, before we use the Bible as binoculars to investigate the lives of others, we need to first use it as a mirror to see ourselves. The problem with religious people is that they use the Bible to judge others, but not themselves. Jesus said this leads to a plank-speck problem where you see the dust in their eye and overlook the gigantic beam in your own. As we study the life

and ministry of Elijah together, please use what the Holy Spirit
is teaching you to examine your own life before examining the
lives of others. This is the best way to be an Elijah and avoid
being an Ahab or Jezebel.

In addition to this book, at RealFaith.com/Elijah you
can find the following additional free resources on the life and
ministry of Elijah:

→ 11 Sermons on 1 Kings 17-2 Kings 2 in audio and
   video format, along with sermon transcripts and
   sermon notes from the series "New Days, Old
   Demons: A Study of Elijah"
→ An 11-week Bible study guide and commentary
   "New Days, Old Demons: A Study of Elijah" that
   covers 1 Kings 17-2 Kings 2.
→ Daily Devotions for the "New Days, Old Demons:
   A Study of Elijah" series.
→ In the Real Men section at RealFaith.com, there
   are also four special bonus sermons on passive
   Ahab and controlling Jezebel focused on men
   understanding how to be an Elijah at home
   and work

I want to personally thank everyone who prays for us
and partners with us to get Bible teaching out to the world as
quickly, cheaply, effectively, and creatively as possibly. This book
is self-published so it cannot be cancelled, has no endorsements
so that no one else can be attacked, is free in digital format,
and available in print for a gift of any amount with all proceeds
going to RealFaith to get more Bible teaching out so that my
motives for writing it are clear. This is the most popular sermon
series I have preached since I became a senior pastor in 1996,

and I believe the truths I'm sharing are the most anointed and prophetic, so thank you for giving me the honor of sharing them with you.

A voice in the desert,

Pastor Mark Driscoll

God Creates,
Satan Counterfeits

In the ancient days preceding the prophet Elijah, in places where God had been worshipped, there started appearing large demonic images of bulls. These tributes were to the demon god Baal, the archenemy of the Lord and a god worshipped for wealth.

Following the stock market crash of 1987, in 1989 near Wall Street, Baal again appeared. To this day, the image of the bull, stands as a symbol of strength and virility, power and money, just as the worship of Baal always has. The bull is 11 feet high, 16 feet long,  weighs 7,100 pounds, and is curiously golden just like the idol created by people to worship demons in the days of Moses, now representing hopes of blessing us with a bull market.[b]

For too long, too many people have read the Bible as if it were a primitive, outdated, and unhelpful view of the world. C.S. Lewis referred to this common hubris as "chronological snobbery", as if we have evolved beyond the fools' parade of history that preceded us. The truth is, while we have evolved externally, we have not evolved internally. We have more modern amenities and technologies around us, but we are no more loving, kind, truthful, or healthy than generations that preceded us. In this book, we will examine how old demons are back doing evil in new days. No longer hiding in the shadows, they are unblushingly in plain sight for those who have eyes connected to a renewed mind.

In the ancient and modern world, Baal was and is worshipped for wealth and power. As the god of the rain, it was believed he would make the crops grow, which fed the livestock, which together sustained human life and grew the economy. Baal was so popular in the ancient world, that the Bible speaks against this powerful demon and archenemy of God over 100 times. Often, you will see the name "Baal" followed by another name that is for a local city or region. Entire cities and regions named themselves in tribute to Baal, and today it would be spiritually accurate to rename cities like Baal-Seattle, Baal-Portland, Baal-San Francisco, Baal-Chicago, Baal-New York, Baal-Washington D.C., etc. Today, the worship of Baal is manifest in the lust for power and money at any cost.

In the ancient world, Jezebel is the demonic mother of prostitution, pornography, and pleasure. Ancient art depicting her is vulgar, crass, and pornographic. She had sacred prostitutes who were influencers in their day like porn stars and underdressed social media mavens in our day who are worshipped as goddesses. In the ancient and modern world, Jezebel is about taking sex which should be in marriage out of marriage, should be private into the public, should be for adults to children, and should be done in love instead for profit. Jezebel turns sex into a religious counterfeit by "offering your body as a living sacrifice to the gods". The Jezebel spirit continually erases any sexual boundaries, and, in our day, is pressing for legalized prostitution, polygamy, and the removal of any meaningful age of consent as children are being sexualized at a young age in school curriculum and on social media platforms. The result is a fast-increasing sexual abuse of minors, which is proven to increase the rate of gender confusion and transgenderism. In their *Youth Risk Behavior Surveillance Survey*, the Center for Disease Control also confirms that sexual abuse and related trauma experienced in childhood causes sexual dysfunction, the mental health problem of gender dysphoria, unhealthy behaviors such as increased promiscuity, and obviously pornography addiction.[c]

Together, these demons have overtaken Western culture at every level (political, educational, spiritual, financial, etc.). They are no longer hiding in the shadows but instead operating in plain sight because we have given them dominion over cultures and nations through our sin. Baal and Jezebel worked together in the ancient world as the highest-ranking demons presenting themselves as male and female. To worship these demons included sexual sin of every sort and kind, removing sex from marriage and childbearing, creating a cultural of monetizing sex, sexual addiction, and child sacrifice. In the West, this began with the sexual and cultural revolutions of the 1960's in everything from sex to drugs, no fault divorce along with legalized abortion and Jezebellian feminism of the 1970's, Baalistic materialism and consumerism of the 1990's, increase in cohabitation and dependence upon government along with the decline in church attendance in the early 2000's, to the complete culture war now playing out online with more division and deception along with temptation than ever before. Anyone who believes the Bible, or even traditional values, is labeled a heretic, and attacked by a demonic mob. This is precisely what happened in the days of Elijah, and we are now also living in the demonic days of Elijah.

Hell is Hot, and So are Demons Today

While church attendance and the percentage of people professing to be Christians has been trending down for years, the
demonic counterfeits are more popular than ever as spirituality
and entertainment has grown darker and more sinister. *Newsweek* says, "Pew Research reported that 62 percent of American
adults believe in Hell, up from 58 percent in 2014, and pop
culture appears to be taking full advantage of the curiosity that
surrounds Hell and its inhabitants. The Devil is front & center in
movies, TV shows, podcasts & even children's books. There are
Satan After School Clubs…There's *The Exorcist Files*, in which
Father Carlos Martins recreates exorcisms, and the podcast
routinely tops the list of the most popular in the 'spirituality'
categories. On Netflix alone there are dozens of titles dealing
with hellish demons, including *Warrior Nun*, *Devil in Ohio*, *The
Bastard Son* and the *Devil Himself and Lucifer*, in which the
ruler of Hell runs a piano bar in California. Comedy is also fair
game, thus Ted Danson plays a torturous demon who is prone
to mistakes in the Netflix series, *The Good Place*…Humans crave
spirituality, says Martins [host of *The Exorcist Files*], but a Gallup
poll in 2021 noted that for the first time in U.S. history less
than half of all Americans were members of a church, synagogue
or mosque. To fill the void, many are embracing 'a rejection of
received social customs and expected behavioral norms in favor
of embracing "me-first" pleasure, pursuing intense feelings and
experiences,' Martins told *Newsweek*. 'The adoption of Satan as
a figurehead is merely another 'shock' ceiling through which the
movement has broken through.'"[d]

God Creates, Satan Counterfeits

Throughout the Bible, God creates and Satan counterfeits. Genesis 1:1 says, "In the beginning, God created…" 2 Thessalonians 2:9-10 [NLT] speaks of, "the work of Satan", as, "counterfeit power and signs and miracles. He will use every kind of evil deception…"

In the homes our children lived in when they were little, all our light switches were simply on and off. Some years into our marriage, we were able to purchase and move into a newer home which had more modern amenities that were new to our children. For example, our kids were used to light switches that were simply entirely on or off. However, our newer and more modern home had multiple rooms where the lights were on a dimmer switch. Our children could often be found playing with the dimmer switch. They found it quite amazing to be able to control the lighting on a range from dark to light.

One of the primary metaphors the Bible uses to describe spiritual warfare is light versus darkness. God wants His people to live in the light, and Satan wants us to live in the darkness. Much like a dimmer switch, Satan and demonic forces know that if they simply flipped everything from light to darkness, it would be too obvious and stark. So, evil forces at work in the world slowly turn things darker and darker hoping that, over the course of years and generations, the darkness is winning without being alarming. This is precisely the backdrop for the ministry of Elijah—things had grown dimmer and darker for generations, and Elijah came to turn the light on.

Demonic counterfeits are often referred to as "false" throughout the Scriptures and include everything from false teachers to false prophets, false apostles, and false teaching. Christian discernment is the ability to rightly distinguish between that which God creates and that which Satan counterfeits. In the book *Win Your War* that I wrote with my wife, Grace, we delve deeply into this reality of spiritual warfare and give numerous examples including angels vs demons, truth vs lies, Spirit-filled vs demon-possessed, humility vs pride, forgiveness vs bitterness, worship vs idolatry, shepherds vs wolves, Spirit vs flesh, church vs world, and Heaven vs Hell.

The backdrop of the life and ministry of Elijah is spiritual warfare as God is seeking to sustain His Kingdom that He created, and Satan is at work through a succession of demonic kings creating a counterfeit kingdom to tempt God's people away from worship and into idolatry.

God was very clear about His commands for kings to worship Him alone and serve as the worship leader of His people. God says in Deuteronomy 17:14–20:

> *"When you come to the land that the Lord your God is giving you, and...say, 'I will set a king over me, like all the nations that are around me,' you may indeed set a king over you whom the Lord your God will choose. One from among your brothers you shall set as king over you. You may not put a foreigner over you, who is not your brother...And he shall not acquire many wives for himself, lest his heart turn away, nor shall he acquire for himself excessive silver and gold.*
> *"And when he sits on the throne of his kingdom, he shall write for himself in a book a copy of this law, approved by the Levitical priests....and he shall read in it all the days of his life, that he may learn to fear the Lord his God by keeping all the words of this law and these statutes, and doing them, that his heart may not be lifted up above his brothers, and that he may not turn aside from the commandment, either to the right hand or to the left, so that he may continue long in his kingdom, he and his children, in Israel."*

In disobedience to God, King Solomon built the Temple for the worship of God, and sadly took many foreign wives who turned his heart away from God, eventually causing him to sanction and support the worship of demonic false "gods" that included child sacrifice, the same murderous act of modern-day abortion.[1] After the death of Solomon, his kingdom was divided into two parts—the northern kingdom (Israel) and southern kingdom (Judah). Keeping this fact in mind is helpful when studying the Old Testament because there is division between God's people and two kings and kingdoms from this point forward in history. In some ways, the situation would be akin to what America would look like had the Civil War resulted in one nation in the north and a separate nation in the south. For Israel and Judah, both kingdoms had numerous evil kings who despised God and deceived God's people.

---

1   1 Kings 11:1-13

THE GREAT SEA

MT. HERMON

LEONTES R.

TYRE

PHOENICIA

•DAN

ARAM

•APHEK

JEZREEL
•

RAMOTH-GILEAD

ISRAEL

GILEAD

SAMARIA•

TIRZAH
•

JORDAN R.

PENUEL

SHECHEM

BETHEL•

AMMON

JERUSALEM

PHILISTIA

JUDAH

•BEER SHEBA

ARNON R.

MOAB

ZERED R.

EDOM

THE DIVIDED
KINGDOM

50 KM

0

50 MILES

Angels and Demons

Throughout the story of Elijah, there is the appearance of both angels[2] and demons or "gods",[3] including named demon gods like Baal and Asherah.

There is only one true God, Yahweh, the Creator of Heaven and earth[4] and all other "gods" are no more than powerful angels, spiritual beings who can do supernatural things[5] but are "nothings" when compared to Yahweh.[6]

The Old Testament clearly states that there is only one God[7] and the New Testament is in full agreement.[8] The Bible also teaches that there is no one like God,[9] thus, claiming to be like God is a satanic lie.[10] However, demons (fallen spirit beings) may also pose as gods and elicit worship, possibly even through counterfeit signs, wonders, and miracles. This is precisely what happens in the book of Exodus and is also the backdrop for Elijah's ministry in a spiritual war against these counterfeit demon gods working through a godless king and false prophets.

These "gods" are very powerful fallen angels and other spirit beings who rebelled against God. They revile the real God and want to replace him with gods. Practically, this means that there are incredibly powerful demonic spirits, with names such as Baal

2   1 Kings 19:5,7; 2 Kings 1:3, 15

3   1 Kings 19:2, 20:10, 20:23

4   2 Chronicles. 15:3; Jeremiah 10:10; John 17:3; 1 Thessalonians 1:9; 1 John 5:20–21

5   Exodus 7:11-12

6   Deuteronomy 32:21; 1 Samuel 12:21; Psalms 96:5; Isaiah 37:19, 41:23–24, 29; Jeremiah 2:11, 5:7, 16:20; 1 Corinthians 8:4, 10:19–20

7   Deuteronomy 4:35,39, 6:4–5, 32:39; 1 Samuel 2:2; 2 Samuel 7:22, 22:32; Psalms 86:8–10; Isaiah 37:20, 43:10, 44:6–8, 45:5,14,21–22, 46:9

8   John 5:44; Romans 3:30, 16:27; 1 Corinthians 8:4–6; Galatians 3:20; Ephesians 4:6; 1 Timothy 1:17, 2:5; James 2:19; Jude

9   Exodus 8:10, 9:14, 15:11; 2 Samuel 7:22; 1 Kings 8:23; 1 Chronicles 17:20; Psalms 86:8; Isaiah 40:18,25, 44:7, 46:5,9; Jeremiah 10:6–7; Micah 7:18

10   Genesis 3:5; Isaiah 14:14; John 8:44

and Asherah who are center stage in life of Elijah, along with other named demon gods such as Chemosh, Molech, Brahman, Jezebel, Allah, Mother Earth, Mammon (money), and Aphrodite (sex), that are wrongly worshiped by multitudes as gods. One major theme of the Bible is that God creates and Satan counterfeits. False gods are behind false religions led by false teachers who perform false miracles - all schemes to lead people astray from the real God to the false gods.

Bible teachers have tended to simply refer to everyone in the unseen realm as angels. The Bible does speak of angels a lot— some 300 times in roughly 90 percent of the books of the Bible. There, we learn about "innumerable angels"[11] and "thousands upon thousands [and] ten thousand times ten thousand".[12] Only two angels are named—Gabriel the messenger and Michael the warrior. There are also categories of angels like archangel and commander which denote senior leaders, and also kinds of angels such as cherubim and seraphim. Angels are also referred to as "stars" and "morning stars" because they are between us and the heavens spiritually like the stars are physically. Angel means messenger, and angels are most likely lower-level divine beings in God's divine family.

In addition to angels, however, there are also numerous other divine beings referred to throughout Scripture as "watcher", "holy one", "holy ones", "host of heaven", "Prince of the host", "Prince of Persia", "chief princes", "man clothed in linen" and a "lord". When God's divine family gathers, they are referred to as the "divine council", "assembly of the holy ones", "the council of the holy ones", "hosts", "the seat of the gods", "the mount of assembly", "the court...in judgment", and "the heavenly host". It was the divine council that met with Jacob travelling down a

---

11   Hebrews 12:22

12   Daniel 7:10

ladder at Bethel (meaning house of God), and it was the divine council that Daniel, Isaiah, and John reported seeing gathered around Jesus on the throne in the unseen realm.

There is also long-standing error within biblical scholarship interpreting the Old Testament word "elohim" as one of the names for God. The problem is that the word is not only used of God, but also numerous other divine beings which leads to the faulty conclusion that the Old Testament is polytheistic with many gods.

The spiritual realm has rank and hierarchy.

Dr. Michael Heiser explains, "The fact that biblical writers label a range of entities as 'elōhîm that they elsewhere take pains to distinguish as lesser than Yahweh tells us quite clearly that we ought not understand 'elōhîm as having to do with a unique set of attributes possessed by only one Being. A biblical writer would use 'elōhîm to label any entity that is not embodied by nature and is a member of the spiritual realm. This 'otherworldliness' is an attribute all residents of the spiritual world possess. Every member of the spiritual world can be thought of as 'elōhîm since the term tells us where an entity belongs in terms of its nature. The spiritual realm has rank and hierarchy: Yahweh is the Most High. Biblical writers distinguish Yahweh from other 'elōhîm by means of other descriptors exclusively attributed to him, not by means of the single word 'elōhîm..."[e]

When the demonic queen Jezebel vows her loyalty to the "gods", this is the precise word she is using. In so doing, she is giving her undying allegiance to a created being, a fallen angel, rather than to the Creator God.[13]

A simple way of summarizing all of this is to say that

---

13   1 Kings 19:2

any being in the divine realm is referred to in the Bible as an "elohim". That includes God and other divine beings. Psalm 82:1 is one clear example of this principle, "God [elohim] has taken his place in the divine council; in the midst of the gods [elohim] he holds judgment."

From the beginning, God's people have lived with constant pressure to accept other religions and "gods" as equally worthy of worship as the God of the Bible. Too many times people are like Solomon and divide their devotion between God and the "gods".[14] His failure to remain devoted solely to God set in motion the splitting of two kingdoms and the succession of demonic kings that we will study next. To embolden us, the Bible presents stirring stories of faithful followers like Elijah and Elisha who would not compromise their devotion to God despite facing opposition and persecution.

Israel's Evil Kings

Just prior to the entrance of Elijah in 1 Kings 17, the scene is set with the reporting of the demonic kings who became increasingly evil with every generation in the northern kingdom of Israel.

King Jeroboam, we are told in 1 Kings 13:33, "...did not turn from his evil way, but made priests for the high places again from among all the people. Any who would, he ordained to be priests of the high places." 1 Kings 14:16 speaks of "...the sins of Jeroboam, which he sinned and made Israel to sin."

King Nadab's brief reign is reported in 1 Kings 15:25-26, "Nadab the son of Jeroboam...he reigned over Israel two years.

---

14   1 Kings 11

He did what was evil in the sight of the Lord and walked in the way of his father, and in his sin which he made Israel to sin."

King Baasha killed Nadab and murdered all the descendants of Jeroboam.[15] God rebuked Nadab saying in 1 Kings 16:2-4, "...you have walked in the way of Jeroboam, and have caused my people Israel to sin, provoking me to anger with their sins, therefore, I will consume Baasha and his house... Anyone belonging to Basha who dies in the city the dogs shall eat; and anyone of his who dies in the field the birds of the air shall eat."

King Elah's short worthless reign is reported in 1 Kings 16:8-10,13, "he reigned two years. But his servant Zimri...conspired against him. When he was...drinking himself drunk... Zimri came in and struck him down and killed him...because of all the sins of Baasha and the sins of his son Elah that they committed, and that they caused Israel to commit, provoking the Lord God of Israel to anger with their idols."

King Zimri's short and sick reign is reported in 1 Kings 16:15-19, "...Zimri reigned seven days...Now the troops... heard it said, 'Zimri has conspired, and he has killed the king'; therefore all Israel made Omri, the commander of the army, king over Israel that day in the camp. So Omri went up...and all Israel with him, and they besieged Tirzah. When Zimri saw that the city was taken, he went into the citadel of the king's house; he burned down the king's house over himself with fire, and died—because of the sins that he committed, doing evil in the sight of the Lord, walking in the way of Jeroboam, and for the sin that he committed, causing Israel to sin."

King Omri established Samaria as the new capital instead of Jerusalem. 1 Kings 16:22-26 says, "...Omri became king...he reigned for twelve years...He bought the hill of Samaria...he fortified the hill, and called the city that he built, Samaria...

---

15   1 Kings 15:27-32

Omri did what was evil in the sight of the Lord; he did more evil than all who were before him. For he walked in all the way of Jeroboam...and in the sins that he caused Israel to commit, provoking the Lord, the God of Israel, to anger by their idols." Samaria was considered so accursed by God's people, that for the next nearly thousand years, devout believers from the north would travel around Samaria to avoid the Samaritans until Jesus Christ told the famous parable about the Good Samaritan,[16] was falsely accused of being a demon-possessed Samaritan,[17] and walked through Samaria to sit down with a woman at a well who became an evangelist to the Samaritans.[18]

The message is clear—things can always get worse, and government is usually the problem, not the solution.

King Ahab, we are told, is the worst of the worst in 1 Kings 16:29-33, "...Ahab the son of Omri reigned over Israel in Samaria twenty-two years... Ahab son of Omri did evil in the sight of the Lord more than all who were before him. And as if it had been a light thing for him to walk in the sins of Jeroboam son of Nebat, he took as his wife Jezebel daughter of King Ethbaal of the Sidonians, and went and served Baal, and worshiped him. He erected an altar for Baal in the house of Baal, which he built in Samaria. Ahab also made a sacred pole. Ahab did more to provoke the anger of the Lord, the God of Israel, than had all the kings of Israel who were before him." 1 Kings 21:25 concludes, "There was none who sold himself to do what

16   Luke 10:25-37

17   John 8:48

18   John 4

was evil in the sight of the Lord like Ahab, whom Jezebel his wife incited."

The message is clear—things can always get worse, and government is usually the problem, not the solution. This haunting historical backdrop sets the stage for the entrance of Elijah. According to a Bible commentator, "The prophet Elijah prophesied to Israel, the northern kingdom, during the tumultuous reigns of King Ahab (874–53 bc) and King Ahaziah (853–32 bc)."

In every age, including Elijah's and our own, there are too many politicians and too few prophets. Politicians tell people what they want to hear, prophets tell people what they need to hear. Politicians are worried about keeping their power, prophets are worried about honoring their God. Politicians are covert, and dishonest, prophets are overt and honest. Politicians say what they want, prophets say what God wants. Today, as much as in the days of Elijah, we need far more prophets and far fewer politicians. This is especially true in the church where the politicians too often get onto the board, into the pulpit, or running the denomination. Elijah serves as a courageous and fearless example of a prophet who keeps having the head on collision with the politicians.

Civil Disobedience

Throughout the story of Elijah, the men of God (Elijah and Obadiah), defy the government and practice what is known as "civil disobedience". Civil disobedience is what true believers must do when the government either commands them to do something that God forbids or forbids them from doing something that God commands.

In the days of Elijah, when Ahab and Jezebel had the churches closed, Bible-teaching schools outlawed, prophets killed, and commanded the worship of Baal and Asherah, there was no choice but to obey God and disobey the government.

According to the Bible, human authority is derived from God and not innate in self. God has all authority, and He delegates it to politicians, parents, pastors and others along with commands regarding how they are to exercise that authority. When a person in authority abuses the authority God has given them, using it in a way that is sinful and against God's commands, their authority is negated.

Believers should not be rebellious, anti-authority, or lawless, as a general rule, because our God prefers order over anarchy. However, when the government is wrongly exercising authority in an evil manner, believers often understandably struggle to make difficult decision of whether to obey or disobey. One Scripture that is perhaps most often (mis)quoted in these instances is Romans 13:1, "Let every person be subject to the governing authorities. For there is no authority except from God, and those that exist have been instituted by God." The first half of the verse declares that those under authority should honor that authority. The second half of the verse declares that those in authority should honor God's authority over them. A person under ungodly authority needs to remain loyal to God as their highest authority, hence civil disobedience. This explains why Paul not only wrote this Scripture, but also got arrested and convicted by the government numerous times, even writing four New Testament books from prison for practicing civil disobedience.

Civil disobedience is a frequent act of worship to God through godly people in the Bible. In Egypt, the Hebrew midwives would not kill babies, allowing Moses to live, grow up, lead the Exodus, and write the first five books of the Bible. In Babylon, Shadrach, Meshach, Abednego did not bow down to worship the image of King Nebuchadnezzar. It is believed that roughly 300,000 people bowed to worship an idol (including many professing believers), while only three stood up literally sticking out like a sore thumb. In Persia, Daniel prayed publicly when King Darius outlawed it. In the days of the early church, Peter and the disciples were commanded not to preach Jesus (4:18) and did so against the law saying in Acts 5:29, "We must obey God rather than men."

Lastly, the Lord Jesus Christ was killed by the Roman Government by welcoming people to honor Him by declaring "Jesus is Lord". In that day, a Roman citizen was welcome to worship any deity they wished, so long as they declared, "Caesar is Lord". The highest allegiance was to be to the national political leader, or what is commonly called "emperor worship". The government executed Jesus Christ, at least in large part, for what they considered an act of civil disobedience by placing Himself above the government. The truth is, God is above the government and many corrupt and demonic governments seek to overtake the Church and replace God as the highest authority. This is precisely the backdrop of the life and ministry of Elijah, a spiritual warfare case study in civil disobedience when government declares war on God.

In our day, this lesson is vital. For example, as various states in America demand that parents of children with gender dysphoria give them puberty blockers, start them on a lifetime of hormones, and mutilate their genitalia if that is what they minor child wants or risk losing custody and having the child seized by the state to be medicated and mutilated, their response must be civil disobedience. The Bible is clear that marriage is for one man and one woman, and that Christian couples have male and female children that they are supposed to raise as sons and daughters. Anytime the government tries to override and overrule God, believers are forced to practice civil disobedience to government in Christian obedience to God.

As some "Christian" denominations slide into apostasy and false teaching on closed-handed, historically-essential Christian doctrines (e.g. male and female gender, marriage solely for one man and one woman, full authority of the Bible as God's Word, need for sinners to repent of sin to be saved, etc.), there will need to be Christians who leave their churches and churches that leave their denominations to honor God. When a denomination of churches, or a local church, is disobedient to God, a godly Christian must be obedient to God.

For example, during COVID, when some governmental agencies in Canada forbid churches from gathering, surrounding the buildings with fencing, and worshippers tore the fences down to enter the church and worship the Lord, it was the right thing to do. As anti-Christ lawmakers throughout the world increasingly seek to restrict Bible preachers from teaching the whole counsel of God's Word or punish Christian churches and ministries for not embracing same-sex marriage, there must be godly and orderly civil disobedience as we see in Elijah's constant conflict with godless government.

Elijah's Miraculous Ministry

As the world grows spiritually darker, we can find a great encouragement and example in the life and ministry of Elijah. In the midst of dark and demonic decline, one man stepped onto the stage of history from prior obscurity. We are not told about

Elijah's parents, upbringing, education, or much of anything else. All we are told is that he was from "Tishbe in Gilead". Tisbhe is apparently such a small ancient town that, to this day, we don't know exactly where it was. Elijah started as literally a no one from nowhere. His name means, "My God is Yahweh".

Gilead is a region known as a remote place of refuge. It was home to rugged mountain men who enjoyed the privacy of the desolate and rocky hill country. The people living there generally lacked social etiquette and educational credibility. There is a television show called "Alone" where outdoor survivalists are dropped into remote areas with only a few items utterly alone. They must build shelter, obtain water, hunt food, and manage a fire to remain alive. The person who can endure this rugged lifestyle the longest without tapping out emotionally or physically each season is declared the winner. Elijah would have easily won this show. At one point, he even hiked roughly 100 miles of rugged terrain through the heart of Asherah worship while on Israel's "Most Wanted" list to visit the widow and her son at Zarephath. Elijah was a rugged mountain man and looked every bit the part. 2 Kings 1:7 describes the reported sighting of Elijah the unpolished prophet, "He said to them, 'What kind of man was he who came to meet you and told you these things?' They answered him, 'He wore a garment of hair, with a belt of leather about his waist.' And he said, 'It is Elijah the Tishbite.'" In many ways, Elijah and his successor many years later, John the Baptizer, are brothers in spiritual battle. Matthew 3:4 reports, "John wore a garment of camel's hair and a leather belt around his waist, and his food was locusts and wild honey."

How Elijah got a meeting with the evil king Ahab we will never know. A man of few words, he makes it clear that a battle is brewing between the powerful demon Baal, worshipped by

Ahab, and the One True God, "the LORD, the God of Israel."
Like Jesus who would later stop a storm by the sheer power
of His word, Elijah prophecies that rain will not fall for three
years until he prayed to God for rain to fall again. A man of
few words, God has Elijah openly and publicly starting a fight
with Baal, who was worshipped as the god of rain and who was
believed to control the seasons, crops, and fertility. In addition to
prophesying, James tells us that his power came from praying.[19]

Most of what we know about Elijah is found in 1 Kings 17
and the report of his spiritual war against King Ahab and his
demonic wife Jezebel. Elijah was a prophet with a prophetic
name that foreshadowed his ministry. Eli means "strength of the
Lord", and Jah means "my God is Jehovah". Together, Elijah
means "I live by the strength of the Lord my God". Simply
stated, the Holy Spirit sustained Elijah to live beyond his natural
limitations to live a supernatural life.

The power of the Holy Spirit at work in and through
Elijah is staggering as his life is a series of miracles. A miracle
is, "An event that defies common expectations of behavior and
subsequently is attributed to a superhuman agent; an occurrence
that demonstrates God's involvement in the course of human
affairs."[9]

A miracle occurs when God overrides natural laws and
does what is often described in the Bible as a "sign", "wonder",
or "power" that is otherwise impossible. Those with an atheistic
view of the world as a closed system devoid of God are natural-
ists. Christians, in contrast, are supernaturalists.

Deism is the false teaching that that a god made the
universe but then left his creation alone and has no dealings
with it, a bit like an absentee landlord. With a god absent,
deism teaches that the world runs by natural laws that a god

19   James 5:17-18

established to govern his creation. Subsequently, miracles are impossible because the universe is a closed system, and a god does not intervene in his creation or overrule his natural laws. This is a commonly held belief and explains why scenes like the fire strike from Heaven to protect Elijah are often rejected as myth or dismissed as primitive ancient suspicion. However, the worldview of the Bible is that there are two realms—seen and unseen—that form one reality. God rules over both, and these two worlds world originally were together as one. We see this, for example, when God met with Adam and Eve in the Garden of Eden, which was the connecting point between the realms. Also present was an angel who was ordered to stand guard protecting the Garden once our first parents sinned. When the divine being Satan showed up in the form of a serpent, our parents were not shocked or surprised because, in that place, human beings and divine beings commonly met.

You cannot believe God's Word or understand God's world unless you embrace the supernatural. From beginning to end, the Bible is about an unseen realm as real as the visible world. Faith is required to believe in beings as real as we are who live in a world as real as ours and travel between these worlds, impacting and affecting human history and our daily lives. As a result, everything is spiritual, and nothing is secular. What happens in the invisible world affects what happens in the visible world and vice versa. Furthermore, everyone is both a physical being with a body that is seen and a spiritual being with a soul that is unseen. Spiritual warfare is like gravity—unseen. It exists whether you believe in it or not, and it affects you every moment of every day. This worldview is on full display in this and other scenes of Elijah's life. When we rise from death and enter into God's Kingdom, we will do so with a physical body and a spiritual soul to live in both realms with human and divine beings as God's full forever family.

The entire storyline of the Bible is built upon God creating everything and everyone out of nothing as a miracle.[20] There is a theological belief called "cessationism", which basically says that the supernatural gifts and outpouring of miracles ceased (with possible rare exception), with or very soon after the days of the Apostles. I have never held this position, or understood it, and find it to lead to a downplaying of both the supernatural godly and demonic events in the Bible, as well as providing a less-than-clear picture of God.

Here is a list of miracles in Elijah's life and ministry:

→ God stopped the rain for three and a half years in answer to his prayer (1 Kings 17)
→ The widow of Zarephath's oil and flour were supernaturally renewed daily (1 Kings 17)
→ The widow's dead son was returned to life as the first resurrection in the Bible (1 Kings 17)
→ God fed Elijah with bread and meat, delivered by ravens, twice a day (1 Kings 17)
→ God sends fire from Heaven (1 Kings 18)
→ God sent rain in response to Elijah's prayer after a three-and-a-half-year drought (1 Kings 18)
→ Elijah outran a horse to escape a coming flood (1 Kings 18)
→ God spoke to Elijah in a whisper (1 Kings 19)
→ Fire comes down from Heaven two more times (2 Kings 1)
→ Elijah was taken to Heaven in a chariot (2 Kings 2)

The Bible often refers to a miracle as a "sign" that points to the Kingdom of God when the unseen realm invades the seen

20 Genesis 1-2; Hebrews 11:3

realm. Before sin entered the world, and after Jesus returns to raise the dead and lift the curse, the Kingdom of God will have no sickness or death. Miracles are signs that point us forward in faith to the Kingdom of God ruled by our miracle-working King Jesus! That is precisely what we see, for example, when Elijah visits the home of the widow and her son in Zarephath.[21] God's miracles through Elijah provided their daily bread, as Jesus later prayed, and raised the dead, as Jesus did, pointing them and us to the King and Kingdom. God can and does do miracles today! This is why believers pray for everything from people to be saved, bodies to be healed, provision to be given, and even the dead to be raised. Why? Because God is free to do whatever He wishes, and no one can stop His will from coming to pass.

We will study more about this miracle-working mountain man and his battle as a true prophet with 850 false prophets next.

---

21 1 Kings 17:8-24

True vs False
Prophets

During the COVID season, there was perhaps the most powerful series of false prophecies given in world history by governments, media, and cultural influencers. A demonic spirit of fear gripped the planet. For the first time in world history, the Church of Jesus Christ was closed globally, even on Easter, when the resurrection of Jesus was not widely celebrated on earth for the first time in two millennia. Governments across the earth took on debt in exchange for dependance from citizens, and mental health was crippled for an entire emerging generation. We were told, in apocalyptic terms, that everyone was at risk and deaths would be unfathomable. In retrospect, some people with high risk needed to adjust their lifestyle to guard their health, but the false prophets were not telling the entire truth. In the days of Elijah, it was also a corrupt government employing false prophets to shut down the churches and we now have new days but old demons up to their old tricks.

In the days of Elijah, Jezebel closed the churches and hired 850 false prophets to work for the government to help her cause. In the days of the early Church, the Jezebel spirit sought to control the churches by a "woman Jezebel, who calls herself a prophetess".[22] The demonic Jezebel spirit works through false prophets to close and control churches.

The controlling Jezebel spirit in government and passive Ahab spirit in churches were on full display during COVID-19.

In what may be a harbinger of the last days, the closure of the churches in Israel in Elijah's day was nothing compared to the closing of the Church globally in our day. The Jezebel spirit ruled the governments that demanded churches shut down, and the Ahab spirit ruled the churches who passively complied. The Christian Church is the biggest, longest standing, and most global movement of any sort or kind in world history. Governmental ability to close churches globally, forbidding the public worship of Jesus on earth, would have been unthinkable previously in world history but serves as a painful birth pain.

A few years after the passing of most government restrictions for COVID-19 that allowed the Jezebel spirit to close the Church, the Ahab spirit is now ruling churches. Cowards are in the pulpit and on the boards, preferring to play it safe and be pathetic rather than prophetic. The result is dying churches. Reports consistently reveal that many, if not most, professing Christians have not returned to church, and have no plans to return to meeting together as God's people, but instead have become passive in their faith. Curiously, in Jesus' rebuke of the church at Thyatira over tolerating the Jezebel spirit in Revelation 2, He also warns that people will fall on a "sickbed". There is a connection between tolerating the Jezebel spirit, and widespread sickness. One scholar in the original languages who explains this refers to basically a hospital bed or, "*Pallet, stretcher* on which a sick man was carried", and "a lingering illness as a divine punishment."[h] Churches that do not stand strong against the Jezebel spirit, but instead become weak and woke like the Ahab spirit, become sick and begin dying.

True vs False Prophets

Jesus,[23] Paul[24] and John[25] all promised that false prophets would come. The presence of false prophets in every age suggests that the people of God must always consider how to distinguish the true from the false prophets. The task is difficult since the false prophets claim many of the same qualifications as the true prophets. Like true prophets, false prophets claim to also speak for God.[26] Therefore, simply, just because a prophet claims to speak for God and can perform miracles and wonders does not mean that he speaks for or does these acts by the power of God. Satan can perform false miracles,[27] like when Pharaoh's sorcerers and magicians turned their staffs into snakes, like Aaron had done.[28] In some regards, the story of Elijah is a case study in discerning between true vs false prophets and real vs counterfeit supernatural activity.

Sometimes, false prophets work for the government, and are well paid to promote a narrative that serves and advances a political and economic agenda. In the days Elijah, the 850 false prophets were said in 1 Kings 18:19 to, "eat at Jezebel's table." This simply means that she gave them access, power, and wealth in return for being her pastors and PR firm to lead the masses astray.

A few criteria help distinguish between true and false prophets. A true prophet had outstanding moral character, like

---

23   Matthew 7:15, 24:11,24

24   Acts 20:29-31

25   1 John 4:1

26   1 Kings 22

27   Deuteronomy 13:1-3, 2 Thessalonians 2:9, Revelation 13:13-15

28   Exodus 7:8-13

Some ministries are strong on the Word of God, but weak on the presence of God.

Elijah,[29] while false prophets do not.[30] The prophecy of a true prophet comes true every time, as happened with Elijah.[31] False prophets are for hire and preach what they are paid to preach, like the 850 prophets of Baal and Asherah,[32] unlike Elijah who was very poor and outcast. False prophets prophesy only peace, whereas Elijah preached judgment and doom.[33] The message of a false prophet conflicts with God's prior revelation, led to the worship of false gods and was punishable by death.[34] This is precisely what happens throughout the life of Elijah as he battled the 850 false prophets.

Some ministries are strong on the Word of God, but weak on the presence of God. The teaching and learning are strong, but the worship, prayer, and life in the Spirit is weak. Conversely, some ministries are strong on God's presence but weak on the Word. The worship is powerful, prayer is passionate, and there is a great interest in signs and wonders but too little healthy and accurate Bible teaching. Ideally, Christians, and Christian ministries would be strong in understanding God's Word and living in God's presence by having a personal relationship with the Holy Spirit, who is God's presence among us on earth.

Discerning God's presence is something the believer is constantly learning. Elijah had experienced God's presence in

---

29   Ezekiel 13:10-16

30   Isaiah 28:7

31   Deuteronomy 18:14-22, Jeremiah 28, 1 Kings 22

32   Micah 3:11

33   Jeremiah 6:13-14, 8:10-11

34   Deuteronomy 13:1-5

everything from fire sent from Heaven to an angel ministering to him during a time of spiritual depression and the whisper of God.

Elijah serves as an incredibly healthy and strong combination of Word and Spirit ministry. He is fiercely loyal to the Word of God, filled with the Spirit of God, and aware of the presence of God.

Elijah, A True Prophet

Elijah is called a prophet repeatedly.[35] Over 77% of the Christian Bible is the Old Testament, and roughly 25% of the Bible was prophetic when written, predicting and revealing future events ruled by God.

Numerous terms are used to identify the Old Testament prophet. The title "man of God" refers to their exemplary character and passion for God.[36] One Bible dictionary says that "man of God" in the Old Testament is "A term used primarily for prophets...In the NT the phrase appears in the Pastoral Epistles and in some manuscript traditions of 2 Pet. 1:21. Here the prophetic connotation is absent, and the phrase is used of followers of God, especially leaders in the Church."[i]

The titles "seer" and "visionary" refer to the prophetic experience of receiving a message from God, either by special insight or visions and dreams.[37] The title "prophet" refers to the office of the person chosen by God to both receive from and communicate for Him.[38] The title "servant of the Lord" reveals

---

35   1 Kings 18:22, 36; Malachi 4:5; Matthew 16:14; Mark 6:15, 8:28; Luke 9:8,19; John 1:21, 25

36   Deuteronomy 33:1, 1 Samuel 9:6, 2 Kings 4:9

37   1 Samuel 9:9, Amos 7:12, Isaiah 30:10

38   2 Samuel 3:20, 1 Kings 18:36, 2 Kings 6:12, Haggai 1:1, Zechariah 1:1

the intimate relationship between God and His prophets.[39] The title "messenger of the Lord" refers to the duty of the prophet to speak for God.[40]

In summary, the prophetic calling was the combination of two ministries. First, they received specific revelation directly from God. The Scriptures are clear that the prophetic message was not the result of human speculation, research or opinion but was a completely miraculous revelation from God through His prophets. Second, they communicated that revealed Word, in speaking or writing, to the people God had called them to. The prophets were also painfully aware of the weightiness of their call since they consciously knew that they were the very mouth of almighty God and spoke for God Himself. For example, this is clearly seen in Moses,[41] Isaiah,[42] Jeremiah,[43] Amos,[44] and Zechariah.[45]

Elijah is clearly a true prophet empowered by the Holy Spirit, and he is in spiritual battle against the unholy spirits working through the 850 false prophets of Baal and Asherah who work for King Ahab and Queen Jezebel. The Jezebel spirit at work in the days of the New Testament also claims to be a prophet but is in fact a false prophet according to Jesus Christ, who says in Revelation 2:20-21:

"I have this against you, that you tolerate that woman Jezebel, who calls herself a prophetess and is teaching and seducing my servants to practice sexual

---

39   2 Kings 9:7, 17:13; Jeremiah 7:25; Ezekiel 38:17; Zechariah 1:6
40   2 Chronicles 36:15-16, Isaiah 44:26, Haggai 1:13
41   Exodus 4:16, 7:1-2
42   Isaiah 1:20
43   Jeremiah 1:7
44   Amos 3:8, 7:16
45   Zechariah 7:12

immorality and to eat food sacrificed to idols. I gave
her time to repent, but she refuses to repent of her
sexual immorality."

Elijah is a true prophet working with other true prophets, and
Jezebel is a false prophetess working with false prophets.

Elijah's ministry begins by predicting a three-year drought,[46]
which he later prophecies the end of.[47] Elijah also foretells the
death of Ahaziah,[48] and a plague from God as judgment in the
days when Jehoram reigned as king of Israel.[49] God does supernatural miracles for and through Elijah, including multiplying
flour and oil for the widow who houses him, and raising her
son from the dead.[50] Elijah predicts the judgment and gruesome
death of the family of Ahab, including his wife Jezebel, which
comes to pass as promised.[51] Elijah also receives the "word of the
Lord which gives him divine authority to speak for God".[52] We
are also told that Elijah obeys the word of God, and commands
others to do the same. Others recognize Elijah's relationship
with the word of God, including the widow who says, "Now I
know that you are a man of God, and that the word of the Lord
in your mouth is truth".[53]

Unlike priests who were selected by their family origins,[54]
prophets had only the call of God to legitimize their ministry.
Their call was not predicated upon prior ministry testing

---

46   1 Kings 17:1

47   1 Kings 18:41-46

48   2 Kings 1:2-17

49   2 Chronicles 21:12-15

50   1 Kings 17:17-24

51   1 Kings 21:20-24; 2 Kings 9-10

52   1 Kings 17:1

53   1 Kings 17:24

54   Exodus 28:1, Leviticus 21-22

or ability.[55] This is precisely the case with Elijah, as we know
nothing of his family or life prior to prophetic ministry.

Today, believers can also help discern between true and false
prophets by their inward testimony of the Spirit.[56] Since both a
believing hearer and a true prophet are filled with the Spirit, it is
sensible to assume that the Spirit in a Christian would confirm
that the message was true.

Prophecy exists in two forms today.

One, God can and does reveal the future to His servants
to prepare them for what is coming, often calling people to
repentance of sin to avoid a painful future. These prophecies are
not equal to the Word of God, and should be tested by the Bible,
Holy Spirit, and godly leaders:

→ "Do not despise prophecies, but test everything;
hold fast what is good. Abstain from every form
of evil."[57]

→ "Beloved, do not believe every spirit, but test the
spirits to see whether they are from God, for many
false prophets have gone out into the world. By
this you know the Spirit of God: every spirit that
confesses that Jesus Christ has come in the flesh
is from God, and every spirit that does not confess
Jesus is not from God. This is the spirit of the
antichrist, which you heard was coming and now is
in the world already."[58]

→ "...no prophecy of Scripture comes from someone's
own interpretation. For no prophecy was ever
produced by the will of man, but men spoke from
God as they were carried along by the Holy Spirit."[59]

---

55 Amos 7:14
56 Deuteronomy 18:14-22; John 7:17
57 1 Thessalonians 5:20-22
58 1 John 4:1-3
59 2 Peter 1:20-21

One example of God revealing the future culminated in the purchase of the church building that houses Trinity Church, which our family planted in Scottsdale, Arizona and I preached the sermon series of this book. We had moved to the desert in obedience to God's calling and were awaiting our next ministry assignment from the Lord. Our high school-aged sons called a family meeting one day and said that our kids felt called to plant a church together as a family. So, we started meeting and praying over dinner to plan out our new church plant. The kids named it Trinity Church to honor their grandfather (Grace's father) who planted and pastored a church called Trinity for more than 40 years until he passed away.

To confirm our desire to plant, Grace and I spoke with our overseeing pastors who confirmed God's calling. On one occasion, I met with one of our pastors, Jimmy Evans, and he asked where we planned to meet. I told him I was unsure and that I was looking at possible rental facilities in the city of Phoenix. He then told me that we should not rent but rather wait for the Lord to provide us a building in Scottsdale. With great specificity, he said it would be an older church building, off the 101 freeway, could seat 800, and we would be able to purchase it. Our realtor said no such building was available or had been for as long as he could remember. Then, I got a miracle call that the exact building Pastor Jimmy spoke of was coming for sale off the market. In a series of miracles, we were able to purchase the historic and iconic Glass and Garden church building off the 101 freeway in Scottsdale, which had been named one of the coolest buildings in our valley by a local news outlet. We received the keys on the 50th anniversary to the day of the grand opening (Easter 1966), and held our first informational meeting that evening. The following Easter, we set up as many chairs as possible and our campus pastor informed me that we had 793 chairs set up. I then looked up at the sound booth and there were…7 chairs in the booth for a total of exactly 800 chairs! Over the years, we have done major renovations to the old church, and it serves as a constant reminder that our God knows and rules the future and can reveal it to us if He so desires!

Two, a Bible teacher or preacher who can powerfully and pointedly bring the timeless truth of God's Word to a specific time and need is being used of the Holy Spirit to bring prophetic illumination to their time. This is not a new revelation, but rather a renewed illumination of God's Word. For example, some years ago, I was preaching through the book of Daniel, about the Spirit of Babylon and how it was seeking to close and compromise the church, literally cutting off the next generation with castration. During that series, the COVID pandemic hit, churches were closed, others went woke and apostate with the rise of critical theory led by Marxist efforts at "social justice", and there was a sudden surge of effort in the culture to cause gender confusion for children, including gender mutilation. What we read about in Daniel's day, we saw in our own day, and that book of the Bible had fresh new meaning.

In the history of Israel, the northern kingdom, there were no descendants of David who ruled as king, and none of their kings was godly or righteous. In contrast, eight of Judah's kings in the south were godly and righteous. By the days of Elijah, the northern kingdom was completely overrun by a demonic counterfeit. The demonic kings did not want God's people to travel to the real temple in Jerusalem, and so they established two counterfeit temples with golden calves as the object of worship. This was a direct violation of the Second Commandment, which God gave His people who were guilty of worshipping a golden calf in the days of Moses. This syncretism infuriated God (and still does) and is why He called Elijah to a ministry of troublemaking.

The Prophetic Ministry of Troublemaking

As believers, we eventually find ourselves in the same position as Elijah, admittedly with less at stake. Someone has a problem with God, and God has a problem with them. We are caught in the middle, and when we take God's side, they declare war on us as their enemy and the source of the problem. This is precisely the spiritual war playing out as interpersonal conflict between Ahab and Elijah in 1 Kings 18. After three plus years of losing the battle with God and suffering crippling national drought, one would hope that Ahab had been humbled. No, although circumstances can humiliate us (as they did Ahab), only we can humble ourselves. This is why the Bible says, "humble yourself".[60] Ahab worshipped the demon god Baal who was believed to rule the rain. Yet, it had not rained for three years and, "the famine was severe". Businesses, crops, animals, and people had died in large numbers. Every day was a funeral for the entire nation of Israel, because of the sin of their head, Ahab. Just as Adam's sin as our head brought death to all mankind, so Ahab's sin brought death to all under his leadership. However, he was so selfish that he could not even consider that he was the problem, and that if he humbly repented, then the real God would send the rain and bless the people. He cared nothing for God or others, the very

---

60   Exodus 10:3; 2 Kings 22:19; 2 Chronicles 34:27; Daniel 10:12; James 4:10

two things Jesus told us to love. Instead, Ahab blames Elijah and God, calling him, "troubler of Israel". The word "troubler" is sometimes translated, "asp", or "viper", or basically a serpent like Satan.[j]

Satan is referred to as the "deceiver".[61] Perhaps the worst deception is self-deception. A person who is self-deceived reinterprets everything in their life in terms of a lie. They lose touch with reality, and constantly see themselves as the victim, even blame shifting to innocent people, wrongly accusing them of doing evil. Like Ahab, deceived people are villains, but only see themselves as victims.

Evanjellyfish with no spiritual vertebrae become passive and tolerant.

There is a partial truth in Ahab's word's that Elijah is a "troubler". The problem with the Church today is that being nice seems to be the only criteria for leadership. If a leader acts like everyone is Jesus and every day is Christmas, ever smiling and encouraging, never causing any trouble, we think they are godly. The truth is, sometimes the godliest people cause some holy trouble. Most everyone listed in Hebrews 11 as a hero of our faith caused some holy trouble, along with Elijah who is honored by God for causing a lot of turmoil in an otherwise peaceful and prosperous land ruled by demons. Some years later, the first Christians were accused of the same thing, "Not finding them there, they dragged out Jason and some of the other believers instead and took them before the city council. 'Paul and Silas have caused trouble all over the world,' they shouted, 'and now they are here disturbing our city, too.'"[62]

---

61   Genesis 3:13; 2 Corinthians 11:3; 1 Timothy 2:14; Revelation 12:9

62   Acts 17:6 NLT

Evanjellyfish with no spiritual vertebrae become passive and tolerant, like Ahab, which opens the door to Satan and syncretism like Jezebel, which we will examine next.

Syncretism
Leads to Satan

New York has long been American's largest city, and, for generations, the gateway welcoming new citizens to our nation. The supposed seat of justice in New York is the Supreme Court building.

For generations, the image of Moses sitting atop the building holding the 10 Commandments served as the iconic symbol of justice and the rule of law. In recent years, however, a second iconic symbol has been added. A naked golden Medusa statue in tribute to abortion has been added alongside the Moses statue. Above the people coming to the Court for justice are literally in authority above them tributes to God and a demon.

Historically, the God of the Bible was worshipped in Israel. The public statues, altars, and artwork was devoted to the Lord. When Ahab and Jezebel began reigning in Israel, they removed much of the godly cultural icons and artwork, and instead began a widespread public project of adding tributes to demons alongside tributes to God.

Syncretism Leads to Satan

There was once a hike that I enjoyed because it ended at a pristine river that flowed with clear water rolling over a bed of rocks and after the long, hot, summer hike through the woods, I would take my shoes off, stand in the river, and wash my face with the cool clean water. One day, I arrived at the river to find that the water was muddy and dirty, which ruined the previously Edenic environment. Curious what had polluted the stream, I hiked up the river to find a small muddy creek that was bringing debris from a nearby hill that had been burned in a forest fire and dumping it in the large river. The small muddy creek infiltrated and polluted the entire river. Spiritually, what was happening in the days of Elijah was the same. God wanted pure, clean, healthy worship of Him to flow from His presence in the unseen realm down to and through His people on earth, but the demonic kings of the northern kingdom of Israel had added demonic spirituality to the worship of God, which polluted everyone and everything it touched.

The technical term for this sin is syncretism. One Bible dictionary says, "The term *syncretism* is used by anthropologists and historians to refer to the blending of religious beliefs. This typically occurs when the social circumstances of one group bring them into contact with another. As the two groups interact, members of one group may begin to assimilate aspects of the religious beliefs of the other, resulting in a transformation of the traditional religion. For Christians throughout history, the notion of syncretism has had largely negative connotations and is sometimes associated with heresy. This is due to the fact that assimilation is often perceived as a departure from the purity of the original."[k]

Apostasy is Spiritual Adultery

The result of syncretism is apostasy. Apostasy is, "A public denial of a previously held religious belief and a distancing from the community that holds to it. The term is almost always applied pejoratively, carrying connotations of rebellion, betrayal, treachery, or faithlessness."[l]

The original Greek word for apostasy was derived from treason in battle. A military term, it referred to war when a soldier abandons their nation, betrays their king, and joins the enemy side of the battle. The backdrop of the life of Elijah is spiritual warfare, and those who profess to belong to the God of the Bible while sinning, rebelling, and betraying Him are treasonous apostates. The most famous apostate is Judas Iscariot, who spent three years as a leader in Jesus' ministry, stealing from Him the entire time, and plotting with enemies to murder the King of Kings by the power of Satan, who Judas welcomed to possess him. The demonic kings in the northern kingdom of Israel were a parade of Judases, and their disciples were twice the children of the devil that they were.

In both the Old and New Testaments, God's relationship with His people is described as a covenant that is essentially spiritual marriage. When people are unfaithful to God and start running around with demons, God calls it "prostituting" or "whoring" and calls those who are perverting their devotion "prostitutes" or "whores" depending upon which English translation of the Bible you read. 2 Chronicles 21:13 says, "Ahab led Israel into whoredom..." The language is strong because God wants us to know in the most clear and intense way that syncretism and apostasy is pure evil.

Today, syncretism and apostasy are tragically widespread. The dirty streams of wokeism, deconstructionism, and socialism are continually trying to flow into Christian churches and pulpits. Cults keep trying to add their books to the canon of Scripture. Social justice warriors keep trying to get their godless agendas (often for redefining sex, marriage, and gender) to be virtue signaled with rainbow flags hanging on church buildings. Tolerance and diversity advocates are constantly pressuring Christians to worship and pray with other religions, spiritualities, and ideologies, thereby erasing any lines separating darkness and light.

The God of the Bible demands to be worshipped in the way that pleases Him. The God of the Bible does not permit worshippers to worship in the way that pleases them. At the bottom of all syncretism and apostasy is one simple question—will you worship God how He wants, or how you want? If you don't worship God in the Holy Spirit like Jesus said,[63] you will end up worshipping in the unholy spirits, like Jezebel said.

The Holy Spirit vs the unholy spirits

In our book *Win Your War*, my wife Grace and I delve deep into what the Bible says about angels and demons, including Satan. A few things we highlight include the following.

---

63   John 4:23-24

One, just like in the military, we know the names of those highest in rank, and not those who serve under them. For example, World War II is often referred to as the battle between Winston Churchill and Adolf Hitler. In truth, the men never came to blows, but they did battle through the Allied and Axis powers and the soldiers fighting on each side of the bloody battle. Spiritual warfare works a lot like physical warfare. When we speak of Satan, or any other high-ranking demon, including Ahab or Jezebel, we are not saying that everything evil is done directly by them. In fact, one thing we learn from the story of Elijah is that Ahab and Jezebel get others to do their dirty work. When I speak of the work of Ahab, Jezebel, or any other demon, I am saying that they are functioning like the German dictator Adolf Hitler, Italian dictator Benito Mussolini, and Japanese Emperor Hirohito, evil rulers working together to deploy others to do their dirty work. In the Bible, references to the "strong man"[64] or "prince of demons"[65] convey this very idea.

A dictionary of Old Testament theology says, "Angels in the OT are often ranged in military and astral ranks known collectively as the heavenly host (Deut 4:19; 1 Kgs 22:19), or they are referred to individually as mighty ones. On occasion they intervened in Israel's wars (Judg 5:20; 2 Kgs 6:17). They were led by a captain or prince, who appears as chief angel (Josh 5:14) ...In Daniel the national guardian angels are called... princes (Dan 8:25). The prince of Persia opposes Michael, who is 'one of the chief princes' (Dan 10:13). Michael is also Israel's guardian angel..."[m]

We only know the names of two angels in the entire Bible. These are noted because of their high rank, as evidenced by their crucial missions. One is Gabriel, who brings messages to Jesus'

---

64   Matthew 12:29; Mark 3:27; Luke 11:21

65   Matthew 9:34, 12:24; Mark 3:22; Luke 11:15

parents before His birth.[66] The other is Michael, who is referred to in military terms as an archangel and prince.[67] What is true of war against human enemies is also true of spiritual enemies. Like any army, we do not know the names of most of the enemy troops, as there are many demonic "unknown god(s)".[68]

Just like in wars, only the noteworthy warriors become legends. The Bible names some of these demonic warriors: Baal[69] and other demons working together as the Baals,[70] also called the host of heaven;[71] Ashtaroth/Asherah;[72] Chemosh;[73] Molech;[74] Artemis;[75] Legion;[76] Hermes;[77] Zeus;[78] Dike, also called Justice;[79] Castor and Pollux, the twin gods;[80] Kiyyun, the star-god;[81] the queen of heaven;[82] and Lilith, also called the night creature or screech owl.[83] We also see the princes of Persia and Greece at spiritual war with the Lord's angels.[84]

66   Daniel 8:16, 9:21; Luke 1:19, 26

67   Daniel 10:13; 12:1; Jude 9; Revelation 12:7

68   Acts 17:23

69   Num. 25:1–5; 2 Kings 17:16; 21:3

70   Judg. 2:11,13

71   2 Kings 21:3, 23:4 Judg. 2:13; 1 Kings 15:13; 2 Kings 17:16; 21:3

72   Judg. 2:13; 1 Kings 15:13; 2 Kings 17:16; 21:3

73   Judg. 11:24; 1 Kings 11:7, 33

74   Lev. 18:21; 20:2–5; 1 Kings 11:7; 2 Kings 23:10; Jer. 32:35

75   Acts 19:24–35

76   Mark 5:9, 15; Luke 8:30

77   Acts 14:8–18

78   Acts 14:8-18

79   Acts 28:1-6

80   Acts 28:11

81   Amos 5:26

82   Jer. 7:18, 44:17-19

83   Isa. 34:14, NIV, KJV

84   Dan. 10

New Testament scholar Clinton Arnold has noted that, in addition to the named demons in Scripture, "one scholar has counted 123 different demons identified by name in the rabbinic literature."[n]

Two, God is all-present (*omnipresent* is the theological term) and not limited to a time or place. Spirit beings (angels, demons, and other divine beings), however, are not present everywhere; they are limited to being in one place at a time and must travel from place to place. Because they are created beings, as we are, they are finite like us and not infinite like God our Creator. For example, to bring the news to Mary that she would give birth to Jesus, the angel Gabriel was sent from God to a city of Galilee named Nazareth.[85]

Also, in the days of Daniel, he received a divine vision and was told, "I have been sent to you…for from the first day that you set your heart to understand and humbled yourself before your God, your words have been heard, and I have come because of your words. The prince of the kingdom of Persia [a powerful demon] withstood me twenty-one days, but Michael, one of the chief princes [high ranking angel], came to help me, for I was left there with the kings of Persia, and came to make you understand what is to happen to your people in the latter days. For the vision is for days yet to come".[86] To summarize, God sent a divine being to bring a message to Daniel, but that assignment was stalled by a 21-day spiritual battle with the demonic spirit ruling with the "kings of Persia". The only way victory could happen was for the powerful angel Michel to travel to Persia and engage in the spiritual battle. All of this to say, when we speak of a particular demon (e.g., Ahab or Jezebel), we are holding

---

85   Luke 1:26

86   Daniel 10:11-14

them accountable for the evil that they command lower ranking unholy demonic spirits to do in various times and places.

Returning to the story of Elijah, working powerfully through Elijah against a pantheon of demons is One Spirit—the Holy Spirit. This explains why the Spirit of Elijah is said to have also been at work in and through the prophets Elisha,[87] and John the Baptizer.[88] John the Baptist was even questioned if he was Elijah because his dress,[89] asceticism,[90] ministry in the wilderness,[91] and his bold confrontation and rebuke of an evil political leader[92] all closely mirrored the ministry of Elijah. Jesus' disciples James and John also referred to the Holy Spirit in Elijah by asking Jesus, "Lord, do you want us to tell fire to come down from heaven and consume them?" in reference to the ungodly Samaritans who were descendants of the same people Elijah preached against.

Even Jesus Christ seems to refer to His Spirit-empowered ministry in terms reminiscent of Elijah saying in Luke 12:49, "I came to cast fire on the earth…" Amidst the conflicting reports of who Jesus Christ was, some said in Mark 6:15, "He is Elijah." This correlation between the Holy Spirit's work through Elijah and Jesus Christ makes sense as both multiplied food[93] and raised a dead person.[94] After Elijah raised the dead son of a widow, it is said in 1 Kings 17:24, "Now I know that you are a man of God, and that the word of the Lord in your mouth is truth." After

87   2 Kings 2:15
88   Malachi 4:5-6 cf. Luke 1:17
89   Mark 1:6
90   Mark 1:6, cf. Matthew 11:18
91   Mark 1:4; Matthew 11:7
92   Luke 3:7-14, cf. Mark 6:18
93   1 Kings 17:7; Luke 9:10-17
94   1 Kings 17:17-24, Luke 7:11-17

Jesus raised the dead son of a widow, Luke 7:16 says, "A great prophet has arisen among us!" and "God has visited his people!"

Throughout these examples of Elisha, John the Baptizer, James, and John, and even Jesus Christ, we see the same Holy Spirit who worked through Elijah working through other leaders in such clear ways that their ministry is connected to that of Elijah. Conversely, the same demonic spirits working against the Holy Spirit in the days of Elijah continue their anti-ministry work today, just as the Holy Spirit continues His ministry work today. Bible teachers who prophetically speak the Word of God to the world face the same opposition and obstacles as Elijah. Paul says in 2 Timothy 4:1-5:

> *"I charge you in the presence of God and of Christ Jesus, who is to judge the living and the dead, and by his appearing and his kingdom: preach the word; be ready in season and out of season; reprove, rebuke, and exhort, with complete patience and teaching. For the time is coming when people will not endure sound teaching, but having itching ears they will accumulate for themselves teachers to suit their own passions, and will turn away from listening to the truth and wander off into myths. As for you, always be sober-minded, endure suffering, do the work of an evangelist, fulfill your ministry."*

The Two-Throne Truth

In the ancient Eastern world of the Bible, people squatted, reclined, and sat on the floor. Thrones were reserved for kings who ruled over kingdoms, priests who mediated between people and the "gods" or the real God, judges who rendered decisions regarding sin, and warriors who sat to rest after conquering an enemy and liberating a people.

Throughout the Bible, a throne is mentioned roughly two hundred times, some two-thirds of which are in the Old Testament, with around one-third in the New Testament. Most mentions refer to God's throne, while others refer to thrones of human rulers and Satan. Of the roughly sixty-one appearances of God's throne in the New Testament, forty-five of them are in Revelation. In this great book of Jesus' war to end all wars, God's throne appears in seventeen of the twenty-two chapters, as all human history is a war over who sits on that throne. Surrounding the throne is God's divine council comprised of His two families—human beings and spirit beings—working together as one divine family.[95] Jesus Christ sits upon the throne at the right hand of the Father as our king, priest, judge, and warrior whose sovereign rule extends over all His creation. Seeing Jesus upon His throne reveals His authority, power, majesty, and splendor. Over everything in the book—churches, nations, angels, demons, and saints (living and departed)—is God's throne. God's throne is revealed as the spiritual center of creation and history, the place where all wars started when Satan sought to unseat God and set himself on the throne.

The battle in Israel, just like the war in Heaven[96] was over who got to sit on a throne. Isaiah 14:13-14 says of Satan and demons, "You said in your heart, 'I will ascend to heaven; above the stars of God I will set my throne on high; I will sit on the mount of assembly…I will ascend above the heights of the clouds; I will make myself like the Most High.'"

Before the Great War, there was one throne and God sat on it. Satan and demons sought to remove God from that throne

---

95   Psalm 82:1; Job 38:4-5; Revelation 4-5

96   Revelation 12:7-9

and replace God with Satan. What God creates, Satan counterfeits. Losing the Great War, Satan set up his own "throne",[97]
from which he rules as the "prince of the power of the air, the
spirit that is now at work in the sons of disobedience",[98] and "god
of this world".[99] Seeking to remove and replace God as Lord
over all, Satan and demons continue to make war anywhere and
everywhere they can, seeking to rule over any and every aspect
of culture. This is precisely what Satan did through Ahab and
generations of his family who sat on a throne that was supposed
to honor God's throne, but instead served Satan's throne.

The demonic king Ahab sat on David's throne in Israel.
God had been very clear that David's throne was under His
throne, and anyone who sat on it had to be a Hebrew who
married a Hebrew and lived in obedience to the Word of God
in the fear of the Lord, guarding his heart from the false trinity
greed, pride, and pleasure, while caring for God's children with
the love that he had for his own children and leading the nation
in singular devotion to the Lord.[100] Ahab did exactly the opposite of everything God commanded. Ahab was not God, and
unless he was a servant of God, the real God would remove
him from the throne. Amid the Elijah story, 1 Kings reports this
two-throne truth. The first thrones are occupied by the rulers of
the northern and southern kingdoms, "Now the king of Israel
and Jehoshaphat the king of Judah were sitting on their thrones,
arrayed in their robes" (22:10). The second throne is revealed to
be God's throne in the unseen realm ruling over all thrones in
the seen realm, "I saw the Lord sitting on his throne, and all the

---

97   Revelation 2:13
98   Ephesians 2:2
99   2 Corinthians 4:4
100 Deuteronomy 17:14–20

host of heaven standing beside him on his right hand and on his left" (22:19).

Those who sit in position of power making decisions that impact others positively and negatively are sitting on a throne according to the imagery of the Bible. The decisions leaders make, in everything from politics to education, entertainment, the economy, and church either invite Satan's throne or God's throne to be in authority over their sphere of influence and rule. Those who sit on a throne, be it at the head of the family dinner table, corner office at work, department chair at the university, or standing behind the pulpit in church are either inviting Heaven down to bless people or pulling Hell up to break people. "Hell up" is what happened in the days of Ahab, and what is happening in our own day.

Thin Places

Before sin entered the world, the two realms formed one reality. The physical and natural world human beings live in was connected to the spiritual and spiritual world angels and other divine beings live in. This explains why we see Adam and Eve in the Garden with God, an angel, and Satan, who also appeared. The Garden of Eden was a thin place between the seen and unseen realms. The ancient Celtic Christians referred to places that God's presence was uniquely strong as "thin places", those times and places where Heaven was a bit closer to earth.

The Bible mentions numerous thin places. Jacob also had a visit from God, angels, and the divine council in Genesis 28:10-17. They came down a ladder to meet with him and he said to them, "How awesome is this place! This is none other than the house of God, and this is the gate of heaven." Jacob then named that place Bethel, which means "house of God", because it was at least temporarily the meeting place of God's divine council and the connecting place for the two realms and two families of God. When God met Moses at the burning bush, he was told to take his shoes off because he was standing on holy ground. Both the Tabernacle,[101] and Temple,[102] were thin places meant for God's people to meet with God in worship and prayer. The body of Jesus Christ is a thin place, the literal connecting point between Heaven (the unseen realm) and earth (the seen realm). Today, the body of a Christian filled with the Spirit is also a bit of a thin place.[103] When the church gathers to worship and pray, Revelation 5 reports that, like incense, those acts arise into the throne room of God where He is also being worshipped in the unseen realm.

In the life of Elijah, there were numerous thin places. Elijah is kept by God at a brook in Cherith where he is divinely protected and provided for by the first food delivery service in the form of a raven.[104] God met with Elijah atop a mountain, a common thin place in the Bible.[105] When God comforts and restores Elijah in the wilderness, this too is a thin place.[106] When God takes Elijah to Heaven in a chariot, this is an obvious thin place.[107] Some years later, Elijah also came down from Heaven with Moses to meet with Jesus and His disciples as yet another thin place.[108]

---

101 Exodus 26

102 1 Kings 3

103 1 Corinthians 3:16

104 1 Kings 17

105 1 Kings 18

106 1 Kings 19

107 2 Kings 2

108 Matthew 17:1-13

As we have established, what God creates, Satan counterfeits. This explains why there are also sinful and evil high places and other places in the Bible devoted to the demonic. In the days of Elijah, this included the establishment of the new demonic temple devoted to the worship of Baal and Asherah in Samaria. Another example is Mount Carmel where God sent fire to the very public demonic high place devoted to Baal worship.[109] Also, when God sent him around one hundred miles to "Zarephath, in the land of Sidon" to minister to a widow and her son, Elijah was in the very heart of Asherah worship known for demonic counterfeit activity.

By living in the demonic, Ahab and Jezebel lived a bit closer to the darkness of the counterfeit in the demonic unseen realm. This explains their incredible power for evil.

By living in the Spirit, constant prayer, and the will of God, Elijah lived a bit closer to the unseen realm and its power than most of us do. To encourage us to live our lives in the thin places, James 5:17 (NLT) says, "Elijah was as human as we are, and yet when he prayed earnestly…" The only way to defeat the demonic, as Elijah did, is to live in the Spirit. We will apply this principle to our present day next.

---

109 1 Kings 18

The Ahab and
Jezebel Spirits
Fly Rainbow Flags

In recent years, the Disney that most of us remember has been replaced with an aggressive, progressive, and regressive agenda to indoctrinate young children through evil entertainment.

For their first 65 years, Disney was governed and guided by their "4 Keys" which were safety, courtesy, show, and efficiency. In 2020 Disney added a "5th Key"—inclusion. Even though, for the past few years, you could not work for Disney unless you got the COVID jab (exclusion), most any sexuality and gender identity would be included.

As a reminder, the Jezebel spirit seeks to dominate an organization with a controlling sexual agenda and looks for Ahab-spirited people who will tolerate her agenda by not seeking to stop her. This is precisely what Latoya Raveneau, executive producer for Disney's Television Animation explains saying, "In my little pocket of Proud Family Disney TVA, the showrunners were super welcoming...to my not-at-all-secret gay agenda...I felt, that sense of 'I don't have to be afraid to have these two characters kiss in the background.' I was just, wherever I could, adding queerness... No one would stop me, and no one was trying to stop me."°

Suddenly, Disney employees were not allowed to speak of ladies and gentlemen or boys and girls at their theme parks. The Disney+ platform removed movies like *Dumbo, Peter Pan, The Aristocrats, Swiss Family Robinson, Lady & the Tramp*, and *The*

Jungle Book for being offensive. However, Disney+ did support a cartoon called, "*Little Demon*." The storyline is that a woman gets

pregnant by Satan, and her 13-year-old daughter is the antichrist. The voice of the antichrist girl is a pagan who said, "I love that we are normalizing paganism."[p]

In the days of Noah, God set a rainbow in the sky after flooding the world in judgment for sin, including sexual sins, as a promise that He would not bring a universal flood ever again. In the ancient world, when a warrior would cease from war, it was customary for him to hang up his bow. God said the rainbow was His public way of doing the same.

Curiously, in mockery of God, the rainbow is today the virtue signaling icon for sexual rebellion against the Word of God. If you see a rainbow flag, for example, hanging on a church, in a business, or displayed on someone's social media, they are openly and publicly declaring that they do not agree with or abide by the sexual restrictions God commands. We see this especially during Pride month, which is dedicated to tolerating and celebrating what we should be repenting of. Rather than believing in binary gender categories of male and female, marriage being solely for one man and one woman in a consummated and faithful covenant, and sex solely intended for the marriage covenant, those in our day wanting to defy all of this simply fly the rainbow flag.

The spirit behind this attitude it nothing new. Every generation has new people, but the same demons. This explains why we see the same evils from one generation to the next. Old days, new demons.

King Ahab and Queen Jezebel

When King Ahab married Jezebel, she was young, beautiful, sensual, and pure evil. Their marriage united the kingdoms of Israel and Tyre and welcomed the demonic into Israel. Jezebel's father was the Sidonian King Ethbaal[110]. The ancient historian "Josephus, drawing his information from the historian Menander, states that Ithobalus, an alternate form of the name Ethbaal, was a priest of Astarte who gained the throne by assassinating Pheles, king of Tyre..."[q]

Jezebel's father's name literally means "with Baal" and "enjoying his favour and protection".[r]

Jezebel was born into a completely demonic family under a generational curse with a father who was with Baal and worshipped Asherah as a pagan priest (Astarte is another name for Asherah). This explains why she quickly used her position as queen of Israel to destroy the worship of the real God and demand the worship of demonic counterfeit deities. The incredible demonic power wielded by Jezebel is because, for generations, her family had worshipped demons and done evil. A family under demonic generational curses grows more evil and more adept at doing evil generation after generation as the counterfeit to the blessings that God bestows on families who walk in the Spirit for generations.

Jezebel was a fiercely independent woman, adept at controlling and manipulating her passive husband, King Ahab. She is the kind of woman who does not respect any authority, including male authority, especially the authority of her husband. In the spirit of modern-day feminism, Jezebel's name means, "'un-husbanded", which explains her complete disregard for her

---

110 1 Kgs 16:31

husband as she seeks to unseat and usurp in order to be the head of their marriage and household.[s]

Instead of being married to her husband, Jezebel's highest allegiance and authority was the demon Baal. The name Jezebel is, "perhaps derived from Phoenician name meaning 'Baal is the prince.'"[t]

Jezebel had a Temple (along with numerous other shrines and worship sites) built in Israel devoted to the worship of the demonic counterfeit god Ashtoreth (also called Asherah, Ashtart or Astarte). She also funded 450 demonic counterfeit priests for Baal, considered the king of demons, as well as 400 priests for Ashtoreth, considered the mother queen of demons.[111] The large demonic temple in Samaria was often filled with overflowing crowds of worshippers, as Ahab and Jezebel had the altars (worship centers like churches today) torn down and replaced with shrines and temples to demons masquerading as gods and goddesses.

True believers and God's prophets were persecuted and killed, Bible teaching schools for the prophets were closed, and biblical faith was on its death bed in Israel. The same demonic spirits are at work today seeking to close the church, control the education of children, and cancel any Spirit-filled Bible preacher who would dare speak out as Elijah did. The godly Obadiah hid a few remaining prophets of God in the limestone caves of Carmel, feeding and protecting them at the risk of his own life. There were only 7,000 Spirit-filled leaders who had not "bowed to Baal".[112] Elijah was unaware that he was not alone but still stood up against everything and everyone opposed to God.

In today's terms, Ahab and Jezebel practiced deconstruction

111 1 Kings 18:19

112 1 Kings 19:17-19

and were spiritually progressive. In my book *Christian Theory vs Critical Theory*, I explain:

> "Unlike building something, which is hard, breaking something is easy. As a young man and still to this day, if you give me a crowbar and a sledgehammer, I can dismantle most anything. Traditional theory is basically how we build things. Christianity would fit in with the concept of traditional theory. How do you build law and order? Our God is a God of law. His Word is filled with laws. How do you build a family? Scripture talks about husbands and wives, and it has specific things to say to both as it assumes God-assigned roles for our biological sex, gender identity, and sexuality. What's the best environment for raising a child? God made marriage and He made us male and female to marry, and then increase in number to fill the Earth, subdue it, and parent, raising our children in the admonition and instruction of the Lord according to Scripture. The Bible tells us about the basic principles for economics and private property theory, as not everything should belong to the government, and that stealing something you don't own is a sin. Simply stated, the Bible is a Traditional Theory. It is about how to build things like families, societies, theologies, economies, and legacies.
>
> Critical Theory is basically how we break things that other people have built. It is a sledgehammer in the form of an overarching ideology or worldview that comes to dismantle pretty much anything that was previously built in a culture. Traditional Theory is about construction. Critical Theory is about demolition.
>
> Because we live in a fallen, flawed world and everything is built by someone who is imperfect and flawed, everything that is built has flaws. Every

organization, every institution, every family, every discipline has imperfections because it's architected by imperfect people. And even if there were a perfect system, it would become imperfect because sinners would be running it. That was the case with Adam and Eve. God gave them a perfect world and they wrecked it by acting sinfully. It's much easier to be one who is critical of those who are building than it is to actually build something. It's very easy, for example, to criticize a leader rather than to actually lead people... Critical Theory fits like a glove on the hand of beta males [Abasolom] who live online and critique people who are doing things. From a safe distance, they can pontificate on the ways they felt that a leader could have done a better job, but curiously don't ever leave the house to show us how it's done. God works through Traditional Theory. Our God is Creator, Sustainer, and Redeemer who is about building perfectly, and then faithfully rebuilding what sin has broken. Satan works through Critical Theory. Satan comes to steal what others have created, kill life in the Spirit, and brutally destroy whatever and whomever God loves."

Ahab's passive tolerating of Jezebel led to the deconstruction of life in Israel, and replacement with a new and progressive vision liberated from God, Scripture, tradition, and healthy male leadership in the home and church. Tolerance, diversity, freeing "victims" from systemic oppression caused by patriarchal religion, and the worship of a male deity called "Father" would need to be replaced in every sphere of society from marriage to parenting, gender, sexuality, church, education, politics, and entertainment.

Demons and Denominations

Today, the demons are up to their old tricks in many "Christian" denominations. Numerous formerly Christian denominations are being overrun with a Jezebel agenda. Ahab leaders are doing nearly nothing to slow down the spiritual war for the pulpits and souls of many churches.

Soft-woke pastors seen to be the majority in what I'd call "Evanjellyfish-ism" that lacks any theological vertebrae. They agree with Jezebel but are too cowardly, like Ahab, to just come out of Satan's closet and say it plainly. This was perhaps no more obvious than the recent spiritual tsunami called, "Black Lives Matter". A terrific title with a terrible agenda, the Jezebel spirit working through three co-founding lesbians pushed an anti-god woke agenda while Ahab leaders in politics, education, entertainment, and the church stood by quieter than Adam in the Garden.

In my book *Christian Theology vs Critical Theory*, I explain:

"While preaching through Romans during the heat of the 2020 presidential election between Donald Trump and Joe Biden, I posted the mission statement directly from the website."

The clip of that sermon quickly reached a few million people on just one social media platform and then was completely throttled...Eventually, the mission statement was rewritten, and it has been very difficult to find the original mission statement as a cleansing of sorts has possibly happened online in an effort to take a radical fringe movement and rebrand it as a more marketable and palpable secular cult. The original statement is as follows with my commentary in brackets:

'We make space for transgender brothers [note the borrowing of biblical language] and sisters to participate and lead. We...do the work required to dismantle cisgender [God-given biological sex] privilege and uplift Black trans folk, especially Black trans women...We build a space that...is free from sexism, misogyny, and environments which men are centered...We dismantle [note the language of deconstruction] the patriarchal practice [husbands lovingly leading homes] that requires mothers to work "double shifts" so that they can mother in the private even as they participate in public justice work [replacing husbands and fathers with governments]. We disrupt the Western-prescribed nuclear family structure...We foster a queer-affirming network. When we gather, we do so with the intention of freeing ourselves from the tight grip of heteronormative [male/female] thinking, or rather, the belief that all in the world are heterosexual (unless s/he or they disclose otherwise).'

The cofounders of BLM Alicia Garze, Patrisse Cullors, and Opel Tometi have been open about their own nontraditional gender and sex lives, along with promoting and supporting, "queer and trans folks... along the gender spectrum" according to the about section of their updated blacklivesmatter.com website.[v] This helps explain why, as adweek has reported, "LGBTQ Pride Festivals are Becoming Black Lives Matter Protests."[vi]

Of course, unbelievers without the Spirit have always followed the demonic spirit of this world and lived according to the flesh. We do not expect unbelievers to act like believers. However, God expects there to be a bright line between His Kingdom and the World. Leaders over God's people are supposed to honor God by representing His Word, will, and ways to the people. In this way, the Church is supposed to be like a boat. A boat is supposed to float on and pass through the water, without letting the water into the boat, eventually sinking it. When the Church starts filling up with the world, God sends forth prophets and judgment to purify His people as a witness to the nations shining light into the darkness. This is happening not only in our day, but in every day, including the days of Elijah.

Baal and Asherah

As we've established, the backdrop of the life and ministry of Elijah is spiritual warfare. God was trying to construct His Kingdom, and demons were trying to deconstruct it and replace it with the kingdom of darkness. In Ephesians 6:12, we are taught, "we do not wrestle against flesh and blood, but against the rulers, against the authorities, against the cosmic powers over this present darkness, against the spiritual forces of evil in the heavenly places." People come and go, but the demons at work behind the scenes remain the same, as well as the Holy Spirit who works in and through the true servants of God. Today, the same demonic powers remain at work in the world, seducing people into the same traps that they have always set. In the days of Elijah, king Ahab was the embodiment of the demon Baal, and his wife Jezebel was the embodiment of the demon Asherah. This couple literally worshipped these demons, funding and promoting their worship in Israel.[113]

Ashtoreth or Asherah (also known as Venus) is the Canaanite goddess of fertility and sex, often worshipped with

---

113 1 Kings 18:19

her male counterpart Baal, with sex being part of their cultic worship. They were considered king and queen of the "gods" or demons. It was believed they had an intense sexual relationship and liked to be worshipped by people having sex without any limitations. Uncovered ancient monuments to Asherah show her in lewd terms with large breasts. As early pornography, Asherah plaques uncovered by archaeologists explain, "She is always naked and her vagina is always very well articulated."[x] Worship sites built by Jezebel to Asherah included "poles" that were male phallic symbols used to advertise sexual sin of all kinds at these demonic worship sites, "the sacred pole erected as her symbol (1 Kgs. 16:33, 2 Kgs. 13:6)."[y]

Mentioned repeatedly throughout the Old Testament, Baal (usually worshipped with Asherah) was a constant threat to holiness among God's people, which is why numerous prophets speak out against him including Jeremiah, Gideon, Elisha, Hosea, and Zephaniah. Just like our day that has landmarks, icons, and signs to let people know where churches and businesses are, this sex cult had large poles put in the ground atop high places as phallic symbols to let everyone know where to go to find the most sinister sex. 2 Kings 9:22 summarizes all of this speaking of "…the whorings and the sorceries of…Jezebel." She was one of many ancient demons considered the "holy ones" or sacred prostitutes, and idols representing her were often nude and pornographic. God commanded His people to stop sinning at these places, and instead tear them down and burn everything related to it.[114]

Baal was considered by the godless Canaanites to be the god of storms, rain, and the highest-ranking demon in the unseen realm. The fact that Elijah prayed to His God to stop the rain, and it did not rain for three years, was seen as clear defeat

---

114 Deuteronomy 7:5, 12:3; 2 Kings 18:4, 23:6; Judges 6:25-30; Micah 5:14

of Baal.[115] He was worshipped for fertility to crops, animals, and people. This demon was worshipped through sex, and temples devoted to him included uninhibited sex. The worship of Baal included child sacrifice in what were the demonic prototypes for Planned Parenthood clinics.[116] Baal is a continual problem for God's people and appears throughout the Bible by a variety of names, including Chemosh, which was the name used by the Moabites.[117] A Bible dictionary says, "Together with his wife, Jezebel, Ahab and his successors made Baal worship the national religion of Israel. The people worshiped various Canaanite deities alongside the worship of Yahweh as represented by two golden calves (1 Kgs 12:28). However, when Ahab married Jezebel, daughter of Ethbaal, king of Sidon, the couple established Baal worship (1 Kgs 16:30–31), and even persecuted those who worshiped Yahweh as prescribed by the Law (1 Kgs 19:10)."[z]

The same Bible dictionary also says, "Together, the demonic counterfeit worship of Ashtoreth and Baal included all of the various lesser-known demons and occultic activities opposing worship of the only true Creator God. It often appears that Baal worship in the Old Testament is a catch-all description of either non-Yahwistic, Canaanite worship or non-sanctioned religious practice. The case is similar with Asherah, a female deity..."[aa]

The current equivalent of Baal worship would be the radical environmental rights advocates teaching us to listen to and obey Mother Earth so that she will bless us with, and not disobey her or face her punishment through climate justice. Every year, the United Nations (UN) encourages all nations on the earth to celebrate, "Mother Earth Day." Referring to the planet as a living being speaking to us through prophets who can hear and interpret her, we are told by the UN, "Mother Earth is clearly

---

115   1 Kings 17:1; James 5:17

116   2 Kings 3:27

117   Numbers 21:9

urging a call to action... we need a shift to a more sustainable economy that works for both people & the planet. Let's promote harmony with nature and the Earth."[ab]

C.S. Lewis once accused people of "chronological snobbery". What he meant was that we think we are far more intelligent and advanced than the more primitive people who lived long before us. The worship of Baal as the God of the environment, weather, and life-sustaining water and crops has simply been marketed and repackaged by worshipping Mother Earth instead of Father Baal.

Christians Need to Come Out of the Closet

Self-righteous, self-deluded, self-important people who take themselves seriously but not God are sometimes the most difficult to deal with. This is precisely the scene in the showdown on Mount Carmel between the prophet of God filled with the Holy Spirit, and the false prophets filled with unholy spirits.[118] The scene is very public, as this is an evangelistic moment with the masses watching. Elijah does not speak much to the false prophets, instead he speaks to the fearful people. In that day, many of God's people were apostate, lukewarm, and living compromised lives. They saw the religious schools closed, and religious leaders killed, and so they decided to dilute their faith rather than destroy their life. The same is true in every day, including our own. Like Billy Graham at an old school crusade, Elijah was calling the people to a decision saying, "'If the LORD is God, follow him; but if Baal, then follow him.' And the people did not answer him a word."[119]

118 1 Kings 18:20-40

119 1 Kings 18:21

The people did not answer because they wanted to see who won the fight before they declared their allegiance. They were living by sight, not by faith. However, God graciously and patiently pursued them as He does us. In this scene, we learn some important lesson about evangelism.

Our faith is to be public and private.

First, our faith is to be public and private. Since God is Lord over our public and private lives, our worship of Him and witness for Him must be both private and public. Just as Christ was public, so Christians must be public. God could have made it rain without sending Elijah to pick a highly public fight with Ahab and the prophets of Baal, but God wanted this to be settled publicly and not privately. In our day, there remains a great pressure for believers to stay in the closet, while everyone else comes out of the closet. If we love the Lord and people, we must let people know who the Lord is in hopes that He saves them as He has us. Jesus is Lord of our heart, but since all of life flows from the heart, it only makes sense that He is also Lord of all of our life.[120]

Second, some people come to saving faith through persuasion, and others through power. Those who come to faith through persuasion typically have a lot of questions and objections to be answered. Their process of trusting God can be slow, methodical, and filled with research. Those who come to faith through power typically see God show up and do some sort of supernatural miracle that proves to them, through experience, that God is real. In this scene of Elijah's evangelistic ministry, the people will need to see God's power to convert. Like any battle, the terms

---

120 Proverbs 4:23

are publicly stated so that the winner is obvious in the end like in 1 Kings 18:24 as Elijah says, "...you call upon the name of your god, and I will call upon the name of the LORD, and the God who answers by fire, he is God."

The demonic false prophets of Baal and Asherah were invited to go first. As we have noted, Baal was worshipped as the god of the crops, rain, and fire. He had failed at the first two for three years, and now had one final chance to prove himself publicly by bringing down fire to consume a bull as a sacrifice. The prophets of Baal danced, shouted, and cried out to their demon-god for hours. They probably looked like Native American shamans who do something similar when they chant loudly, dance vigorously, and bang poles on the ground in an effort to conjure up demonic spirits from the underworld. This entire scene is witchcraft, the human attempt to control the demonic realm for personal benefit. Despite all the magic and witchcraft, nothing happened because the Lord of all is also Lord of the demons, and He did not permit them to appear. Elijah then mocks the entire spiritual structure of all of Israel under the rule of Baal, accusing their "god" of being constipated and tied up on the toilet all day, unable to make an appearance. One Bible commentary says, "'Elijah was saying that Baal could not respond to his worshipers because he had gone to the toilet.'"[ac]

The false prophets respond by cutting themselves and shedding their blood. This scene is a grotesque counterfeit of what God would do by sending His Son to shed His blood in our place for our sins. The real God does not demand our blood, but rather gives His own. The gospel of Jesus Christ tells us that this counterfeit was trying to deceive people as Jesus shed His blood, and then sent fire down from Heaven on Pentecost. His blood and fire are the truth, and this scene is the demonic counterfeit.

Elijah begins by honoring God through rebuilding the altar which had belonged to the Lord but been destroyed when the worship sites for God were torn down. Elijah than has the entire sacrifice drenched in water (possibly salt water, which was available nearby as fresh water was scarce from the drought), to show God's power without question. Unlike demons, the false prophets sought to control through witchcraft, but Elijah merely prays to God who is free to do as He pleases and cannot be controlled or manipulated by anyone. God then sends fire from Heaven that consumes the bull, the stones, and even the water and dirt. This moment had to look something like a military airstrike from Heaven, exactly on target arriving in an instant, reminiscent of the days when God did the same on Sodom and Gomorrah.[121]

What they really wanted was rain, and what they got was fire. God often works this way, giving us what we need before giving us what we want. The fire they needed came first, and as we will see, the rain they needed came next.

Once again, we see the power of prayer as Elijah's simple prayer is answered by God in power. Stunned, the people fell down and worshipped the Lord. In this instant, it was obvious who the true versus false prophets were, and who the true God was versus the false gods.

Today, although these people no longer live, their demons do. They continue their same work today, as they did in Elijah's day, in everything from politics to business and religion. They continue to oppose, threaten, and even silence those who speak the Word of God truly and boldly as Elijah did. These same spirits cause the same fear in many of God's people as they did in the past. Too many believers are keeping their faith private,

---

121 Genesis 19:24; Luke 17:29

so they don't get in trouble, or become apostate, trying to live somewhere in the middle between God and Baal, as if that were even possible since Jesus said, "Whoever is not with me is against me".[122]

The Ministry of Mockery

How should we respond to evil people promoting demonic beliefs? The same way that Elijah did: with a ministry of mockery. Rather than fearing evil, we should be mocking it. The Bible says we should not mock God,[123] but we should mock those who mock God. This helps others who are watching to not be fearful or led astray by demonic doctrines. The late-night talk show hosts in our day make their living by mocking the things of God, and the people of God would do well to learn how to defend what is right by making fun of what is wrong.

Elijah is a prophet, and mockery is part of prophetic ministry. Surely, people will be offended when we do not honor the gender pronoun of their choosing or take their false religious nonsense like Mormon underwear or transgender bishops seriously, but it's all a joke. Entire books of the Bible, such as Amos, are comedic satire.[ad] Perhaps the most humorous line in Amos 4:1 is where God refers to the female members of the Bashan city council as fat cows:

> *"Hear this word, you cows of Bashan, who are on the mountain of Samaria, who oppress the poor, who crush the needy, who say to your husbands, 'Bring, that we may drink!'"*

---

122 Matthew 12:30

123 Galatians 6:7-8

The Bible also includes names and nicknames to mock God's enemies. Examples include Achan (trouble), Agrippa (causes pain), Balak (destroyer), Careah or Kareah (baldy), Chesed (a devil), Chilion (dying), Eglon (fat cow), Emmor or Hamor (an ass), Esau (hairy), Gatam or Mordecai (puny), Harumaph (flat nose), Irad (wild ass), Jareb or Midian (contentious), Mahli or Mahlon (sickly), Nabal (fool), Naharis (snorer), Nahash (serpent), Og (long neck), Parshandatha (dung), and Sanballat (enemy).

God is said repeatedly throughout the Bible to mock His enemies.[124] Jesus did the same, mocking the religious neatniks of tithing out of their spice rack to be holy while ignoring hurting people and murdering God, sucking in their faces to get points for looking holy when fasting, serving as "blind guides" leading people to hell, and worrying about their outer appearance while their inner life was the tomb of a damned soul. In Matthew 15:1-14, when Jesus mocked the evil religious people, they were "offended"—triggered so badly that someone made fun of all they held dear that they probably would have lived on Twitter whining about their victimhood if it was available in their day.

Renowned preacher Charles Haddon Spurgeon said:

> *"I do not know why ridicule is to be given up to Satan as a weapon to be used against us, and not to be employed by us as a weapon against him. I will venture to affirm that the Reformation owed almost as much to the sense of the ridiculous in human nature as to anything else, and that those humorous squibs and caricatures, that were issued by the friends of Luther, did more to open the eyes of Germany to the abominations of the priesthood than the more solid and ponderous arguments against Romanism... 'It*

---

124 Psalm 2:4, 37:13, 59:8; Proverbs 1:26, 3:34

[humor] is a dangerous weapon,' it will be said, 'and many men will cut their fingers with it.' Well, that is their own look-out; but I do not know why we should be so particular about their cutting their fingers if they can, at the same time, cut the throat of sin, and do serious damage to the great adversary of souls."[ae]

Every day, media and social media is filled with a legion of crazy stories that merit mockery. As one example, our family has taken a vacation multiple times in a medium sized rural town known for farming and hunting. At the local public school, a young female identifies as a "furry". Web MD says, "Furries are people who have an interest in anthropomorphic animals, or animals with human qualities. Many furries create their own animal character, known as a fursona..."[af]

In denying nature and reality, our culture has now decided that one's sex and gender are not fixed and determined by God at birth, but instead fluid and everyone can choose and change their identity at any time for any reason they feel is sufficient. This young woman, who obviously needs mental help, identifies as a cat. Rather than getting her treatment, they instead placed a cat litter box in the girls' restroom for her to use.

This is cat-egorically, cat-aclysmic, and cat-astrophic cat-tiness.

We will do a bit of mocking in the next chapter as we look at passive men, controlling women, and the Ahab and Jezebel spirits at work today as they were in the days of Elijah.

Passive Men and Controlling Women:
The Ahab and Jezebel Spirits Today

Tony and Gina met in college while attending the same church. After dating a few years, they were married and moved out-of-state for job opportunities. They began volunteering in nearly every role needed at a small church, spending hours every week serving. Before long, they knew nearly everyone in the church, and had become close with the leaders. People really appreciated the enthusiasm of this young couple, who were quickly promoted to teaching roles.

Since they both had musical ability, they were soon on the stage. The wife even gave them a title, announcing to the congregation one Sunday that she and her husband were the new worship leaders. The pastoral team assumed it was a youthful error and overlooked the public declaration of official leadership. The couple continued serving, and everything was fine until the wife was corrected in a women's Bible study. She said something minor about the Bible that was incorrect, and the simply accurate correction brought out a defensive and self-righteous religiousness that never dissipated.

Eventually, the couple became the greatest threat to the church. The wife became increasingly controlling and domineering. She would show up for team meetings at the church that she was not invited to or part of, started having people to her home on her turf where she could be in control, and began undermining the long-standing doctrinal beliefs of the church.

Eventually, she had gathered enough women to form her own home Bible study that she taught, handing out books by authors promoting teaching contrary to the church, and a faction formed.

The church leadership sat down with her husband to encourage him to speak with his wife, help her heal up, and get professional help if she was willing to deal with a lot of past traumas that had slowly become known as people got to know the couple. The husband was kind, not defensive, listened, and did not say much. The church leaders assumed that he was on the same page with them. The leaders asked him to come to his own conclusion about his wife, get her help if he thought she needed it, but to not divulge all the details of their conversation to her.

The husband went home and reported everything that was said in the meeting, which set the wick that would lead to the explosion of his wife. She started emailing everyone in the church, attacking the church and leaders on social media, and connecting with larger networks led by others with the Jezebel spirit, collecting unhealthy and wounded people to take turns attacking churches and leaders. The church leaders yet again met with the husband and asked the wife to join him, which she refused, as she was acting completely independently of her husband by this time. The meeting was a replay of the first and, after a few more meetings, it became obvious that he was a passive Ahab who would say and do nothing.

It was later revealed that this pattern started in college. Although they professed to be Christians, she became very sexually aggressive early in their dating relationship, and he enjoyed that very much. However, it caused him to lose his respect and spiritual leadership in the relationship. In the marriage, if he did what she said, she was kind to him, took good care of him, and dealt with anything difficult from making money to having conflicts, and making decisions. He learned early on that if she was in control and he was passive, she was happy, and he was cared for.

Rather than leaving the church, the wife started demanding that the current leadership step down and that her husband be the new pastor. She started telling incredible lies about the church and its leaders, inviting anyone who ever had a problem to come forth and meet with her so she could be their advocate. Eventually, there was some anonymous group represented by this woman who was now growing in control over people in the church. Her husband did not want to be the senior pastor, but he was too afraid of his wife to say or do anything. She knew that if he was the leader, his passivity would allow her to ultimately be in control.

As turmoil rolled through the church, people started leaving, but the leadership was not budging. Suddenly, the wife started reporting various visions, dreams, and words from God confirming her plan to overtake the church. This included quoting Scriptures out of context, which confused new Christians and less mature believers.

Eventually, she started demanding detailed financial information about the church. The leaders wrongly assumed that providing her financial data would be something of an olive branch and bring peace. She quickly demanded more specific church expenses, including the salaries of all staff members. When this request was denied, she declared to anyone who would listen that there was a coverup, funds were being misspent, and the leadership refused to "walk in the light" and be "accountable". All of this took place even though she and her husband had given only a pittance during their entire time at the church.

The church leadership did not resign but did continue tolerating her behavior, assuming that at some point she would calm down and they would go away. That would not happen, because her goal was control and if she and her husband left the church, they would not be in control. The only way for her to have control was to rule the church through her passive Ahab husband or to destroy the church as her final act of control. It took some years, but eventually the church died. Of course, the Jezebel woman took to social media to mourn the death of their church and used the demise of the church caused by her years of attacks as proof that she was right, and the leaders were wrong. She alleged that they should have listened to her and allowed her husband to become the pastor because God would have blessed and saved the church. In typical Ahab fashion, he joined her on social media, talking like a victim about how hurt he was, as they had put in so many hours volunteering at the church and he would have been able to keep it from closing, but he was never given the opportunity, which broke his heart.

The couple gathered some people from their former church into a house church. The wife liked having people in her environment because she was in control. Eventually, she drifted into transgenderism and other sexual and gender confusion. Her husband remained passive, and today they are not really Christians anymore, but more committed to deconstructing all that is wrong with orthodox Christianity and the Church. She does most of the attacking in the form of talking and posting like Jezebel, while he says and does little just like Ahab.

If you've ever been in any church leadership position, you likely have some version of this story in your own experience. The Holy Spirit within Elijah and the unholy Jezebel spirit continue to work and war in the world today. The same is true of the unholy Ahab spirit. Admittedly, the Bible does not expressly state the ongoing work of the same demonic spirit at work in and through Ahab in the same way that the Holy Spirit is not expressly said to work through Elijah. However, it can be seen in the account of Elijah that Ahab was empowered by demons, and that Elijah was empowered by the Holy Spirit. The following are reasons to believe that Ahab was demonically empowered, as the counterfeit to being Spirit-filled (like Elijah) is being demon-possessed (like Ahab).

The Passive Ahab Spirit

We learn several things about Ahab throughout Scripture. First, Ahab is a counterfeit of Jesus Christ, ruling over a completely demonic kingdom, fully devoted to evil. Second, Ahab and his counterfeit religious leaders have supernatural powers, not unlike Pharoah in the days of Moses. Third, people live either by the Spirit, flesh, or demonic according to the repeated teaching of the New Testament and the depth of evil in the life of Ahab is truly demonic. Fourth, Ahab's wife Jezebel is clearly demonically empowered, as we have already established, and so they are a demonic couple aligned for evil. Fifth, in 1 Kings 16:29-33, we are told that Ahab, "did evil in the sight of the Lord more than all who were before him... took as his wife Jezebel...and served Baal, and worshiped him. He erected an altar for Baal...Ahab also made a sacred pole. Ahab did more to provoke the anger of the Lord, the God of Israel, than had all the kings of Israel who were before him." The word "evil" is the same word used to explain the spirit that tormented King Saul.[125] Sixth, Ahab[126] and his wife Jezebel[127] are clearly stated to have worshipped false gods. Seventh, 1 Kings 21:25 says, "There was none who

125 1 Samuel 16:14,15,26, 23; 18:10, 19:9

126 1 Kings 18:24

127 1 Kings 19:2

sold himself to do what was evil in the sight of the Lord like Ahab…" This language strongly indicates that Ahab made a proverbial "deal with the devil" and sold his soul into the service of Satan, much like Judas Iscariot would many years later. In summary, Ahab is not just a man, but an evil man empowered by an unholy spirit.

Continuing the story of Ahab, a theologian explains he was a godless king who allowed Jezebel, his wife, to usurp his authority saying, "The Ahab spirit causes men to be weak as leaders in the home and church (Isa. 3:12). This spirit works with fear of Jezebel to prevent God's order in the home and the church. The result is the destruction of the family priesthood. This is a curse that must be broken before Ahab spirits can be driven out. The curse of Jezebel opens the door for these spirits to operate in a family."[ag]

The reasons that people, like Ahab, tolerate the Jezebel spirit are many.

One, because people with the Jezebel spirit are controlling and powerful, people become fearful of them, which allows a domineering, threatening, and manipulating person to rule your life instead of God.[128] This perfectly explains Jezebel ruling over her husband Ahab.

Two, sometimes the Jezebel spirit is tolerated because there is a benefit that comes to the person who is in an unholy alliance with them. This was the case with Ahab who benefitted from Jezebel—she was beautiful and sensual, their marriage brought him political peace and financial prosperity, and she did his dirty work, including lying and murder to get him a piece of property he desired.[129]

Three, a person with the Jezebel spirit has often experienced

128 Proverbs 29:25

129 1 Kings 21

abuse or even trauma in their life that contributed to their desire to be a controlling person to protect themselves from future harm. Those who are compassionate, empathetic, and understanding can wrongly endure the self-destructive behavior they witness in a person with the Jezebel spirit because they feel bad for the hardships they have experienced in their life. However, the most loving thing to do is not explain or excuse their oppression, but instead help them experience deliverance from it.

Four, a woman with the Jezebel spirit, like Jezebel herself, is difficult to deal with when she attacks a man of God like Elijah. The Jezebel spirit often attacks strong, godly male leadership, especially those who speak the truth of God's Word like Elijah did. A woman with the Jezebel spirit who attacks a man of God will then retort that he was unloving, abusive, and harsh if he stands up to her controlling manipulation. In our culture of victimhood, this kind of false claim is immediately met with an outpouring of support for the woman and attack of the man. This happens frequently in the Christian Church,[130] as well as in the realms of politics and business, which Jezebel ruled over in Israel.

In preaching the series on which this book is based, the phrase I kept telling our people regarding Ahab and Jezebel was, "if you tolerate, they will dominate". I believe remembering that phrase is essential to being ready for the spiritual war that inevitably comes. Also, it's important to note that you have to be very clear with a Jezebel that you are not in agreement. If they make a demand, express a conclusion, or tell you what either they are doing or you should do, they will assume your silence is agreement. Like Elijah clearly spoke in a confrontational way to Jezebel, you must speak clearly and confrontationally to a

---

130 Revelation 2:20

Jezebel spirit. They are so used to winning through bullying and domineering that they will steamroll your silence and so you must not be silent, but instead speak like Elijah by the power of the Holy Spirit. Fear of man[131] is what Jezebels sniff like a dog does fear, and they will use your fear to abuse you.

The Controlling Jezebel Spirit

The Jezebel spirit was at work roughly a thousand years after the actual woman died, doing the very same things in the church at Thyatira that she did in Israel—preaching and teaching lies and false doctrine, encouraging sexual immorality, attacking godly leaders (especially Bible teachers operating with a prophetic anointing to preach truth and call sinful darkness to light), and tolerating and celebrating instead of repenting of sin.[132] The Holy Spirit of Elijah, and the unholy Jezebel spirit continue to work and war in the world today. The same is true of the unholy Ahab spirit.

Speaking of the demonic Jezebel spirit, a spiritual warfare manual says, "The spirit of Jezebel causes wives to forsake the covering of their husbands. It is a Hebrew name meaning untouched, untouchable, non-cohabiting, without husband, adulterous, base, licentious. This spirit is characterized by domination, control, and manipulation of the husband instead of submission to his authority. The spirit of Jezebel also operates in the church with spirits of seduction, fornication, and idolatry (Rev. 2:20). It works with the Ahab spirit in men but hates the Elijah spirit (Mal. 4:5–6). It is a very religious spirit and loves to operate in the church. This spirit has been known to operate in

---

131 Proverbs 29:25

132 Revelation 2:18-29

both males and females. Jezebel was very religious and a devout high priestess of Baal. Athaliah (2 Kings 11:1)—daughter of Ahab and Jezebel who married into the royal family of Judah. She had the same spirit as her mother in usurping authority in the kingdom of Judah, an example of how this spirit is transferred from Jezebellic

The Ahab and Jezebel spirit feed off one another.

mothers to their daughters. These spirits also operate through curses of destruction of family priesthood, destruction of family, and Ahab and Jezebel."[ah]

Adding the story of Ahab, it goes on to explain he was a godless king who allowed Jezebel, his wife, to usurp his authority, "The Ahab spirit causes men to be weak as leaders in the home and church (Isa. 3:12). This spirit works with fear of Jezebel to prevent God's order in the home and the church. The result is the destruction of the family priesthood. This is a curse that must be broken before Ahab spirits can be driven out. The curse of Jezebel opens the door for these spirits to operate in a family."[ai]

The Ahab and Jezebel spirit feed off one another. The Ahab spirit avoids conflict, disagreement, and confrontation. The Ahab spirit is often most entrenched in a person who is insecure, needy, and struggles with "fear of man".[133] This causes their passivity. Sometimes, a shy personality, bad upbringing, or unhealed trauma can make their passivity even more severe. A person with the Ahab spirit is particularly vulnerable to someone with the Jezebel spirit. Because the Jezebel spirit is controlling, domineering, and rules by threat, fear, sexual seduction, and

---

133 Proverbs 29:25

punishment or reward depending upon whether they are obeyed, a person with the Jezebel spirit can easily rule over someone with the Ahab spirit forever, unless they are stood up to, which is exactly what Elijah did. Someone with the Elijah Spirit (the Holy Spirit of God) is particularly hated by the Jezebel spirit because they refuse to tolerate evil.

Whenever there is tolerance of, working around, and making excuses for Jezebel, you know the Ahab spirit is at work. This is simply a codependent relationship that is unholy and ungodly as we see in the days of Elijah and every day before and after. The American Psychological Association (APA) defines codependency, in part, as "the state of being mutually reliant" and "a dysfunctional relationship pattern in which an individual is psychologically dependent on (or controlled by) a person who has a pathological condition…"[aj]

The counterfeit of godly unity is ungodly unity. Just as God works through holy alliances (e.g., Ezra and Nehemiah, Moses and Joshua, Elijah and Elisha, Paul and Timothy), so too does Satan work through unholy alliances against those holy alliances (e.g., Sanballat and Tobiah, James and Jambres, Ahab and Jezebel, Hymeanaeus and Alexander). These are examples of "soul ties". It is defined as "a bond between two individuals. The souls (mind, will, emotions) of individuals knit or joined together. A bond, a joining together of souls for good or evil. There are godly and ungodly soul ties."[ak]

Furthermore, "Soul ties are formed as a result of relationships with people. There are godly and ungodly soul ties. Ungodly soul ties cause a person to be manipulated and controlled by another person, causing the person to live in disobedience to God…

Soul ties will cause:[al]

→ One person to follow another (Ruth 1:14–16)
→ A person to fulfill the desires of another
   (1 Sam. 20:4)
→ A person to surrender his goods to another
   (1 Sam. 18:4)
→ A person to react in anger when the person to whom
   they are soul tied to
→ is attacked (1 Sam. 20:34)
→ A person to protect another in times of danger
   (1 Sam. 20:35–40)
→ Loyalty between a leader and his followers
   (2 Sam. 20:2)."

The holy soul tie between Elijah and Elisha is counterfeited by the unholy soul tie between Ahab and Jezebel. In the days of Jesus, on the night He was betrayed, we see this same thing occur as Jesus, who is God, is surrounded by His holy alliance of disciples, and Judas, who is possessed by Satan, is surrounded by his unholy alliance of demonic religious and political leaders determined to murder Jesus.

Holy soul ties form when God the Spirit brings two believers together for mutual edification to spur one another on to love and good deeds. Unholy soul ties form when demonic spirits bring two people together for mutual degradation to spur one another on to evil and destructive deeds. One of our overseeing pastors once asked me, "Have you ever wondered why people who are evil and never met always seem to find one another to form an unholy alliance?" I said, "yes, I have seen this in the church my entire ministry career, and now online technology seems to connect these people like never before causing digital versions of mobs like the one that Paul faced in Ephesus." He said, "demons know each other, and if they are working through people then the demons who work together introduce the people who they are working through to work together for evil." This insight is profound, shocking, and true. The worst people tend to find one another, form an unholy alliance soul tie, and multiply their evil as the counterfeit of Christian hospitality.

A loving family would be an example of a godly soul tie, along with the intimate oneness shared between a husband and wife as they are "one flesh". An ungodly soul tie is when there is the lack of a boundary in a friendship, romantic or sexual relationship, or between married couples and/or families. Adultery creates an unholy soul tie that is the demonic counterfeit of marriage as 1 Corinthians 6:15-17 says, "Do you not know that your bodies are members of Christ? Shall I then take the members of Christ and make them members of a prostitute? Never! Or do you not know that he who is joined to a prostitute becomes one body with her? For, as it is written, 'The two will become one flesh.' But he who is joined to the Lord becomes one spirit with him." This can include emotional or physical adultery, along with spiritual adultery where the boundary lines of heart, body, and soul between marriages and families are blurred so that there is either adultery of the hands or heart between individuals, couples, or families. This was the very kind of sexual sin that Jezebel was encouraging in the days of Elijah, as well as in the church at Thyatira, and in the church and world today.

Demons in the Bedroom

The gospel of Jesus Christ is about the repentance of sin. Jesus' ministry included preaching repentance of sin, "Jesus began to preach, saying, 'Repent, for the kingdom of heaven is at hand.'"[134]

---

134 Matthew 4:17

The counterfeit message of demonism is tolerance. Today, tolerance remains the primary message being preached by the world. Behind the message of tolerance are the same demons that were at work in the days of Elijah through Jezebel. In Revelation 2:20, Jesus says to a progressive and tolerant church, who were perhaps flying a rainbow flag approved by a transgender bishop, "But I have this against you, that you tolerate that woman Jezebel, who calls herself a prophetess and is teaching and seducing my servants to practice sexual immorality..."

The word for sexual immorality in the original Greek text is "*porneuō*" from which our English words pornography and pornographic are derived. The demonic Jezebel spirit of seduction and temptation often addicts people to pornography and other sexual sins. This includes transgenderism and gender confusion. In the days of Elijah, Jezebel brought about a complete sexual revolution in Israel. Today, the Jezebel spirit has done so since the 1960's, with what was once sexually taboo now mainstream.

Demons are not engendered male and female as human beings like us and are not confined to a physical body as we are. The Bible says that human beings were created male and female[135] but does not say the same about divine beings. Furthermore, God only permits sex in marriage, and human beings marry, but divine beings do not.[136] Demons are, therefore, androgynous or gender fluid. They can occupy and possess a male or female body, which means they live gender fluid on a spectrum. They attempt to seduce people to live in rebellion against their God-given gender, and against the limitations Scripture has for sexual activity only within the confines of heterosexual marriage. In this way, demonic spirits, including Jezebel, seduce people to become like them—androgynous, rebellious, and perverted—which

---

135 Genesis 1:27

136 Matthew 22:29-30; Luke 20:35-36

is the worship of demons, starting with Jezebel, renounced in Revelation 2:20. Conversely, the holy angels are not sexual. This simple fact explains the constant war in the Bible from beginning to end between the sexual temptations faced by believers and God's commands to not yield to those sinful desires. This also explains the widespread worship of Baal (a demon god appearing as male), and Asherah (a demon goddess appearing as female), at worship sites created and maintained by Ahab and Jezebel. At these sites, there was sexual perversion of every kind considered sacred worship acts, the phallic Asherah pole serving as the brand logo, and pornographic images of the nude Asherah and child sacrifice, making this powerful demonic spirituality a combination of church, strip club, and abortion clinic.

Demons not only elicit sexual sin, just as Jezebel promoted with the sexual debauchery celebrated with pride to the demons of Baal and Asherah, but at times demons also occupy or possess a human body to engage in sexual sin as a demonic counterfeit of worship, offering a body as a living sacrifice to an unclean spirit.

This is likely what the Bible refers to saying in Genesis 6:4 saying, "The Nephilim were on the earth in those days, and also afterward, when the sons of God came in to the daughters of man and they bore children to them. These were the mighty men who were of old, the men of renown." The only other appearance of this name in the Bible is after Noah's flood in Numbers 13:33 saying, "…we saw the Nephilim (the sons of Anak, who come from the Nephilim), and we seemed to ourselves like grasshoppers, and so we seemed to them." The word Nephilim literally means "fallen ones", and as such could refer to either sinfully fallen angels or sinfully fallen people. There are three options for who the Nephilim are:

One, the groups mentioned in Genesis and Numbers are different people groups with the same name, as the first group died in the flood.

Two, the same demons are working in and through different people before and after the flood.

Three, these are divine beings seeking to conceive with human beings to create an offspring that is both human and divine. If true, this would align with the concept underlying this book that God creates and Satan counterfeits. This might be the demonic counterfeit of the virgin conception of Jesus Christ, who was born of a human being (Mary) and a divine being (the Holy Spirit).

Biblically, there is a strong case to be made. In his seminal work *The Unseen Realm*, Dr. Michael Heiser delves into this issue deeply. For the purposes of a simple summary, God is a Father with a family in the seen realm (human beings) and a family in the unseen realm (divine beings). Until the sin of angels in Heaven (divine beings), who then joined them in sin on earth (human beings), the two families lived together in one realm. Sin separated the families and realms, although human beings are still connected to the unseen realm (e.g., we have an immaterial soul, and believers are filled with the Holy Spirit), and divine beings are still connected to the seen realm.

The problem in much Bible study and teaching is that it lumps everyone in the unseen realm together as simply "angels". In our book *Win Your War*, my wife Grace and I get into all of this in great detail, but a simple summary will suffice for this book. In that book, we say:

> **"The Bible has a great deal to say about spiritual beings, speaking of them as angels, watchers,**

holy ones, the host of heaven, sons of God, divine
assembly, the gods, morning stars, glorious ones,
and the armies of heaven (Dan. 4:17; Ps. 89:5; Deut.
4:19–20; 1 Kings 22:19; 1 Sam. 1:11; Job 1:6; 38:7;
Deut. 32:8–9; Ps. 82:1, 6; 89:6; Ezek. 28:2; Job 38:7;
2 Pet. 2:10; Jude 8; Rev. 19:14). One Bible dictionary,
speaking specifically of angels, says '"angels" are
mentioned almost three hundred times in Scripture,
and are only noticeably absent from books such
as Ruth, Nehemiah, Esther, the letters of John,
and James.'[am]

Another Bible dictionary says, 'From the Garden of
Eden to the renewed heaven and earth, angels are
found repeatedly throughout the Bible. These beings
are also spoken of as spirits, cherubim, seraphim,
sons of God, [and] the heavenly host.'[an]

No one really knows how many angels exist or if God
ever makes more angels. The Bible, however, is clear:
there are a lot of angels. It uses descriptions such
as 'innumerable angels' and 'a thousand thousands
served him, and ten thousand times ten thousand
stood before him' (Heb. 12:22; Dan. 7:10).

Because they prefer the focus to be on God rather
than themselves, it is not surprising that we only
know the names of two angels in the entire Bible. One
is Gabriel, who brings messages to Jesus' parents
before His birth (Dan. 8:16; 9:21; Luke 1:19, 26) The
other is Michael, who is referred to in military terms
as an archangel and prince (Dan. 10:13; 12:1; Jude
9; Rev. 12:7). Since demons are fallen angels who
counterfeit all that God creates, one of the best ways
to understand the demonic realm is to understand the
angelic realm first."

In the seen realm, human beings are referred to as the "sons of God".[137] Most Christians are well-aware of this, but far less aware that, in the unseen realm, divine beings are also called the "sons of God" and "gods". The Bible is not polytheistic in saying this, as the original Hebrew word Elohim is not a title for the one true God, but instead a broad category in reference to any diving being in the unseen realm:

→ **Psalm 82:1** — "God [Elohim] has taken his place in the divine council; in the midst of the gods [Elohim] he holds judgment."

→ **Job 38:4-7** — "Where were you when I laid the foundation of the earth? Tell me, if you have understanding. Who determined its measurements — surely you know! Or who stretched the line upon it? On what were its bases sunk, or who laid its cornerstone, when the morning stars sang together and all the sons of God shouted for joy?"

The reference in Job precedes the creation of the world, and so the "sons of God" cannot possibly be human beings. These are divine beings, created by God, who were present when God created the heavens and the earth, shouting in worship as the angels (morning stars) worshipped in song.

Returning to the story of the Nephilim to establish a theme in our study of Elijah, there are divine beings, who do not have a physical body or male/female gender like human beings, and do not enter the marriage covenant as human beings do. Some of these divine beings rebelled, fell into sin, and were kicked out of Heaven,[138] and came to the earth.[139] These fallen divine beings (including demons), are at work in our world,

---

137 Matthew 5:9; Romans 8:14,19, 9:26; Galatians 3:26, 4:6

138 Revelation 12:7-9

139 Luke 10:18

as is recorded repeatedly in Scripture, including our study of Elijah, along with holy divine beings (including angels). Angels or demons can appear as male or female when on assignment to human beings.[140] There is no report in Scripture of holy angels being involved in human sex, but there is repeated condemning of the connection between unholy fallen demons and human sex, as is the case in the worship of the demon gods Baal and Asherah under the leadership of Ahab and Jezebel in the days of Elijah. One of the most powerful ways that demons seduce people to worship demons instead of the One True God is to elicit sexual pleasure and sexual addiction in connection with demonic worship. In the story of the Nephilim, the "sons of god" may be fallen divine beings or demons, who seek to appear as male seeking to impregnate female human beings called "the daughters of man".

This could be the report of a demonic counterfeit of Jesus' incarnation. If so, Genesis is a report of a counterfeit incarnation, from children of the divine sons of God and human daughters of men, who survived the flood as God and Satan both rescued their lines. There is a similar story along these lines in the ancient Epic of Gilgamesh, which a collection of stories regarding the Mesopotamian hero and fifth king of ancient Uruk (possibly the oldest city in Iraq). Most scholars accept this as a historical person. The stories about his life include incredible strength, wisdom, and power. He was reported to be the son of the goddess (or divine being) Ninsun, and the man or human being Lugalbanda. He was considered a demigod, 2/3 divine being, and 1/3 human being. He lived at the time of the great Meso-potamian flood. Mesopotamia is one of the numerous ancient

---

140 Genesis 18:2,16; 19:1-22; Judges 13; Zechariah 5:5-11; Ezekiel 9:2; Matthew 28:3; Hebrews 13:2

civilizations, including Babylon, Sumeria, Assyria, the Epic of Gilgamesh, etc., that have Flood stories with similar details:

→ Evil people descending into complete destruction
→ God/gods bring a Flood
→ A large boat as a means of rescue
→ Wife, family, and animals are brought onboard the boat
→ Birds are sent out from the boat
→ People exit the boat and worship God/gods
→ A rainbow appears in the sky.

All of this seems to point to confirmation from ancient sources outside the Bible of a possible partially human, partially divine being living and ruling in the days of Noah.

At the very least, demons will tempt and incite our sinful flesh to willingly sin against God sexually. All of this was tolerated and celebrated in the days of Elijah, and our new days are battling these old demons.

The sad truth is that Ahab and Jezebel thought more clearly about the connection between human sex and the unseen realm than many Christians. Today, our western worldview is so dominated by secular deism, that even some Christians (especially those with cessationistic bad theology) have a hard time conceiving of any meaningful connection between the physical and spiritual worlds. So much of the care of people has been infiltrated, even in the church, with secular thinking that the connection between the body and the soul is too often diminished. The *Diagnostic and Statistical Manual of Mental Disorders* is considered the "Bible" for mental health professionals and has a ton of great information but completely overlooks the soul.

Exactly zero times, in the most eminent clinical resource for the care of hurting people, is their soul ever mentioned.

This same thinking pervades our cultural outlook on sex, as if all that was happening when people take their clothes off is connecting their bodies. It seems most everyone has forgotten that within those bodies are also souls and when bodies connect, so do souls. Just as the body houses a soul, so the soul can house a spirit—either the Holy Spirit of God or an unholy spirit like Ahab or Jezebel. At least this demonic king and queen believed what the Bible said about the connection between sex and spirit, even though they used it for great evil and a doorway to the demonic. This is the underlying worldview battle in the unseen realm playing out in the days leading up to and of Elijah.

Tolerance is Demonic

The Bible rarely mentions tolerance and, when it does, it is God rebuking His people for tolerating sin, usually sexual sin. 1 Corinthians 5:1 says to a tolerant church, "It is actually reported that there is sexual immorality among you, and of a kind that is not tolerated even among pagans, for a man has his father's wife." The English translation of the Bible that uses the word "tolerance" the most is the New Living Translation. It speaks of God not tolerating other religions,[141] injustice,[142] sinful behavior,[143] or teaching based on other religions.[144] In the story of Elijah, the Ahab spirit passively tolerates the activity of the Jezebel spirit, and the same demons remain powerfully aligned

---

141 Exod. 20:5; Deut. 5:9

142 2 Chron. 19:7; Mic. 6:11

143 Ps. 5:4, 101:5

144 Rev. 2:14

in our day, including having an entire Pride month dedicated to them. According to the Bible, pride is not only a sin, but also a powerful demonic force. No less than five times, the Bible speaks of "Leviathan", the serpent or dragon, saying, "He sees everything that is high; he is king over all the sons of pride".[145]

Not only is human sex a connection at the soul level but demons are sexual (unlike angels) and androgynous without a human biological sex and gender. In a word, demons are on a nonbinary sexual spectrum, and they are constantly seeking to conform human beings to their image and likeness with gender confusion, transgenderism, and castration of males, as we will learn next.

---

145 Job 41:34; 3:8; Ps. 74:14; 104:26; Isa. 27:1

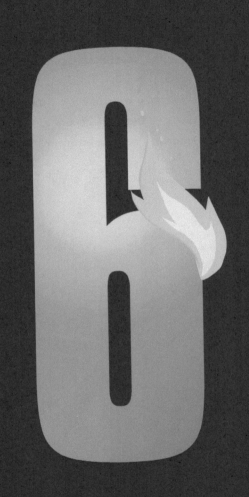

Jezebel is a Transgender
Spirit that Castrates Men

In recent years, there has been a sudden and strong surge of gender dysphoria. In layman's terms, gender dysphoria is the experience of a person who feels psychologically that their gender is different than their physical and biological sex. Simply stated, there is an incongruence between their mind and their body. For example, a man with gender dysphoria will say they feel like, "a woman trapped in a man's body."

The National Library of Medicine asked the question, "Does Maltreatment in Childhood Affect Sexual Orientation in Adulthood?" The medical summary says, "Epidemiological studies find a positive association between childhood maltreatment and same-sex sexuality in adulthood, with lesbians and gay men reporting 1.6 to 4 times greater prevalence of sexual and physical abuse than heterosexuals." The study goes on to summarize research on the issue saying, "Our results suggest that from half to all of the increased prevalence of childhood sexual abuse experienced by sexual orientation minorities compared with heterosexuals may be due to the effects of sexual abuse on sexual orientation, possibly through previously proposed pathways: (1) abuse of boys perpetrated by men causes boys to believe they are gay; (2) abuse of girls by men leads them to be averse to sexual relationships with men; (3) abuse survivors may feel stigmatized and different from others and may, therefore, be more willing to behave in ways that are socially stigmatized, including acknowledging same-sex attraction or having same-sex partners…"[ao]

If people do not get help and healing, they live in brokenness and burden.

To summarize the research that is true but very politically unpopular, the generational surge among younger people toward transgenderism and nontraditional and nonbinary sex and gender roles is largely driven by trauma and abuse. If people do not get help and healing, they live in brokenness and burden. This issue is as spiritual as it is mental and physical. Sin, including trauma and abuse, are an attack on the whole person—and a child enduring evil is affected at every level of their being, which is pure evil. This can include demonic transference from the abuser to the victim who needs to be delivered from ongoing torment through demonic oppression.

With the incongruence between their mind and body, there are three options. One, the person can live with their incongruence, practice sexual self-control, and choose not to act out of their desires to operate apart from their God-given biological sex. Two, they can seek to change their mindset to correspond with their biological sex. Three, they can seek to change their body to agree with their mindset. For example, they can begin to dress and appear opposite their biological sex, or even undergo surgery to change their God-given body to appear opposite of who they truly are.

The latter option is becoming increasingly popular. There is growing pressure in everything from media to social media and government educational curriculum to encourage kids, starting at a young age, to explore the gender spectrum and their sexuality. In some states, schools are not even legally obligated to notify a parent that their child is "transitioning" their sex and gender. We are seeing a rapid increase in gender reassignment surgery, with mounting pressure to do so even on young children, insanely assuming such life-altering decisions as puberty blockers, hormone therapy, and genital mutilation should be made by a child. At work behind this cultural tsunami are the same demonic spirits that Elijah battled in the Old Testament.

Curiously, atheistic lesbian cultural critic Camille Paglia, who has studied in depth the decline and fall of once great civilizations, says that the appearance of widespread approval of transgenderism is at the end of a civilization marking its' impending collapse.[ap] In studying ancient works of public art, for example, she notes that in the early stages of a nation or culture, strong warrior men, often who died for their cause, are honored in the public square with things like statues and paintings. At the end of a culture while it is dying, it is young men who are effeminate and sexualized who are instead highlighted in public, including cultures such as Rome and Greece. It takes the strength of masculine energy to found a nation, start a movement, or create a culture. War and conflict require a high pain tolerance, courage, strategy, and strength. Men create a culture, and women fill it. Much like a family historically, the masculine energy provides for, protects, and houses a woman who then fills the home with love, children, and life. When the men become effeminate, weak, woke, and transgender, the masculine energy that builds is removed and once what was previously built is consumed, the civilization collapses. The mind-melting amount of personal and governmental debt is simply delaying this inevitable crash of a once great western culture that is no longer thinking about the future but only consuming in the present. Today, people are not making sacrifices thinking about the future, but instead killing their children and taking on debt knowing that their present selfish sin will cause future social suffering.

Jezebel's Eunuchs

Surrounding Jezebel at her death were male "eunuchs".[146] It was common for males serving in a demonic pagan government, often as slaves, to be castrated. One Bible dictionary defines it as, "A male servant or supervisory official in the court of a ruler; often castrated."[aq]

It was prophesied by Isaiah that Daniel and the other young men in his day would be taken as prisoners of war and castrated, made eunuchs to serve a demonic king.[147] Since Nehemiah served high levels of government, and no wife or children are mentioned, it is also believed by some that he too was a castrated eunuch. The same demonic spirit may have also been at work in the New Testament church at Galatia. In Galatians 3:1, Paul asks, "O foolish Galatians! Who has bewitched you?" The church had willingly come under the influence of a spirit of witchcraft that had cursed them under a demonic spell. One Bible commentator explains, "No-one believes more firmly than he in the existence and operation of demonic forces (see, for example, Eph. 6:12), but he will not, just because of this, allow the Galatians to shift the blame from themselves."[ar]

Earlier in Galatians, Paul warned about false teachers and prophets saying in Galatians 1:8, "…even if we or an angel from heaven should preach to you a gospel contrary to the one we preached to you, let him be accursed." Galatians is written in large part to contend for the purity of the gospel of Jesus Christ against religious legalism that demanded that the human work of circumcision be added to the finished work of Christ for true salvation. In Galatians 5:12 (HCSB), Paul makes this bold and offensive claim, "I wish those who are disturbing you might also

---

146 2 Kings 9:32

147 Isaiah 39:6-7; cf. Daniel 1

get themselves castrated!" In the region of Galatia at that time, a powerful female demonic counterfeit goddess Cybele was worshipped. One Bible commentary says of Galatians 5:12, "More than one commentator has seen a tacit reference here to the sacral castration practiced by the priests of Cybele."[as] Men who served as priests of Cybele (also called the Anatolian Mother Goddess, Kybele, Agdistis, Rhea, Meter Theon, and Magna Mater) had to castrate themselves and become transgender wearing women's clothes, makeup, letting their hair grow long and styling it like a woman, as ancient drag queens publicly hosting all ages sexualized dances to music.[at]

Denying their God-given masculinity and becoming passive effeminate androgynous beings, this all sounds very much like the passive Ahab spirit and castrating and controlling Jezebel spirit. Some in the transgender and non-binary community actually acknowledge and praise ancient Cybelianism as a source of identification and the "trans god".[au] Today, there are some denominations, like the United Methodist Church, inviting drag queen candidates for ordination like "Ms. Penny Cost" to give the children's sermon in church from the platform, even though "they/them" is a guy named Isaac who wears a dress, wig, and makeup and compares his struggles with the suffering of Jesus saying to overturn injustice.[av]

History of Religions reports, on the "competition between Christian and pagan in the ancient world" as a battle between believers and transgender pagan priests, "These infamous men, with their impure, unchaste, polluted bodies were none other than the galli, priests of the gods Cybele and Attis, whose mystery religion constituted one of early Christianity's major rivals. Time and time again, Christian apologists cited the galli as representative of all they abhorred in pagan culture and religion. And of all the outrages of the galli, none horrified them more than the radical manner in which they transgressed the boundaries of gender."[aw] The correlation between this ancient behavior and our modern day is noted, "as exoticisms equivalent to today's fascination with gender transgression as evidenced by such films as M. Butterfly and The Crying Game."[ax]

History of Religions then reveals that this same sort of combined transgenderism and goddess worship by castrated priests is present in:

> **"the Greco-Roman galli, the priests of the goddess called Inanna in Sumeria and Ishtar in Akkad, and the hijra of contemporary India and Pakistan. The parallels between these priesthoods and the social roles and identities of their personnel are detailed and striking...these priesthoods are largely independent inventions..."**[ay]

If you missed it, the non-Christian academic historical record says that the same thing was happening at different times, in different places, among different religions. Why? The author goes on to speculate and, in the end, cannot come to a coherent and credible solution, because he does not believe in the demonic or the simple fact that demons are not limited to times and places like people are.

The demonic spirit of Jezebel, likely also spoken against by Paul in Galatians, wants men to be emasculated for at least three reasons.

One, this demon promotes gender confusion, hates God's binary gender categories, and celebrates androgyny and gender mutilation. This same demon has fully overtaken much of western culture and infiltrated everything from politics to entertainment, education, and religion. This demon has men competing in women's sports so that men are beating up women in the name of progress and equality. This demon has so won the war that it is now moving to gender confuse and genitally mutilate children openly and unblushingly.

Two, this demon wants men to be passive, powerless, and abdicate their roles of authority so they will tolerate evil usurping and replacing them as leaders and heads over everything from families to churches, governments, and businesses. This same demon has created a generation of men with the lowest testosterone scores on record, encouraged young men to live dependent upon their parents and government, become addicted to pornography, and passively allow the least healthy and most ungodly people to rise and occupy leadership positions in every sphere of society.

Three, this demon is pro-death, not pro-life. Castration is the surest way to negate God's command to be fruitful, multiply, and subdue the earth. This same demon remains at work today in the pro-abortion movement seeking to end human life and flourishing. Castration ensures that a man cannot live as a man or leave any legacy through his progeny. This is the complete opposite of everything God commanded us to be and do before sin entered the world.

God's people have always believed that He made us male and female. The opening pages of Scripture tell us that we are made male and female in God's image, from which we have traditional binary gender categories.[148] Progressives who pretend to be Christians somehow say they agree with Jesus but forget that He quoted Genesis 1:27 as unchangeable fact.[149] This is why the Bible has specific instructions to men and women, including husbands and wives. This is also why God wants men and women to dress male and female as Deuteronomy 22:5 (NASB)

---

148 Genesis 1:27

149 Matthew 19:4; Mark 10:6

says, "A woman shall not wear a man's clothing, nor shall a man put on a woman's clothing; for whoever does these things is an abomination to the Lord your God."

The Old Testament repeatedly forbids God's people from engaging in this androgynous sexual idolatry that had nearly erased the worship of the true God in the days of Elijah.[150] In the very days of Elijah battling these demonic forces, we read in 2 Kings 22:44,46, "Jehoshaphat also made peace with the king of Israel...And from the land he exterminated the remnant of the male cult prostitutes who remained..."

Also, on Mount Carmel the 450 demonic prophets of Baal, 1 Kings 18:28 says, "cried aloud and cut themselves after their custom with swords and lances, until the blood gushed out upon them." Three things are noteworthy. One, when Baal is worshipped, people mutilate their healthy body for no reason but to appease the demons they are devoted to. Two, when people worship Baal, mutilation of the human body becomes a regular and public "custom" common in the culture, and a means of encouraging others to do the same. Three, the cutting and mutilating of the body is a demonic counterfeit of the flogging and crucifixion of Jesus Christ, which is abhorrent to God because our God does not demand our blood, but instead gives His own. The current trend of gender mutilation and cutting of the body being publicly paraded and encouraged is a form of ancient Baal worship.

---

150 Deuteronomy 23:17; 1 Kings 14:24, 15:12; 22:46; 2 Kings 23:7; Job 36:14

The Twisted Trinity of Sex, Gender, and Sexuality

In my free e-book *Christian Theology vs Critical Theory:*

> *"According to the Bible and the general consensus of western scholarship until the sexual devolution of the 1960's and 70's, sex gender and sexuality were fixed and related categories.*
>
> → *Sex: Biological status of anatomically male or female (sex chromosomes, gonads, internal reproductive organs, external genitalia). In babies .1%-.2% have ambiguous external genitalia, and between 1-2% less severe ambiguity.*
>
> → *Gender: The Bible and tradition says that gender flowed from sex with masculine males and feminine females starting from birth so that boys and girls would dress differently and appear differently with things like hairstyles. Today, gender is considered to be determined by how someone feels, not how they were created, which explains males saying they feel like a female trapped in a man's body. Furthermore, the Bible assumes binary gender categories when it speaks directly to men and women, along with husbands and wives categorically.*
>
> → *Sexuality: The Bible teaches that your sexual interest is supposed to be directed toward the opposite sex with heterosexual monogamous marriage as the only hearth intended to house the flames of sexual passion.*
>
> *Today, the Critic's theory is that sex, gender, and sexuality are in no way interrelated. Your gender is not chosen by God in the binary categories of male and female, but the individual now replaces God and gets to assign their own gender on a fluid spectrum*

if they feel that God sinned against them, confining them to the wrong body. This can include gender reassignment surgery, which is how people become their own creator. The Critic imposed this upon Daniel in Babylon, having him castrated so that he could no longer live as a heterosexual married male enjoying sexual relations with his wife and having children raised to serve the Lord. Furthermore, the act of 'coming out' is the public declaration of our identity and allegiance, which is the counterfeit of Christian baptism."

This powerful demonic cultural movement is nothing new and extends from the days of Jezebel to every day that same spirit has been at work in every culture. When we see very similar common sinful and demonic activity in nations, cultures, religions, and periods of history, we must keep in mind that, while people come and go, the demons remain the same. Paul says in Ephesians 6:12, "...we do not wrestle against flesh and blood, but against the rulers, against the authorities, against the cosmic powers over this present darkness, against the spiritual forces of evil in the heavenly places." In our book *Win Your War*, my wife Grace and I explain:

"Paul wrote some of the most focused biblical passages on the war with the demonic realm. His goal was to equip local churches because they are on the front lines of the war. These are the terms Paul uses when describing the "rulers of this age" (1 Cor. 2:6, 8), the rulers "in heavenly places" (Eph. 3:10), and "the ruler of the authority of the air" (Eph. 2:2). Paul often interchanged these terms with others that are familiar to most Bible students:

→ *principalities (archē)*

→ *powers/authorities (exousia) § powers (dynamis)*

→ *dominions/lords (kyrios)*

→ *thrones (thronos)"*[az]

The days of the early Christian Church in the Roman Empire faced different people but the same demons. *History of Religions* says, "References from the first century by Ovid, Seneca, Persius, Martial, Statius, and others, indicate the galli [castrated transgender pagan priests worshipping a female demon goddess] were by then a common sight throughout the empire. In [a]...second-century fable...they are portrayed... they went out, wearing various colored undergarments with turbans and saffron robes and linen garments thrown over them, and every one hideously made up, their faces crazy with muddy paints and their eyes artfully lined...yellow shoes on their feet... they leapt about shouting...raving in a religious dance...whirl their hair hanging around in circles...[and] the cutting [of their arms]...the soil became wet with the filthy blood of the effeminates."[ba]

If this sounds like a public Pride parade that culminates with drag queens counterfeiting the shedding of Jesus' blood, it is because this is precisely what was happening roughly 2,000 years ago. History reports, "At the time of the birth of Christ, cults of men devoted to a goddess flourished throughout the broad region extending from the Mediterranean to south Asia."[bb]

God entered into all this demonic deception as a heterosexual man working a masculine job and controlling His sexual urges. Furthermore, the early Church battled the same demons as Elijah and Paul as progressives claimed to profess faith in the God of the Bible, while worshipping with sexual sin and transgenderism, just as in the days of Israel and Rome. Sounding like "churches" with rainbow flags flying, we are told, "...the relationship between Christianity and the Cybele religion...is more complex than one of simple antagonism... In some cities, worshippers clashed in the streets when the festivals of the two religions coincided, as they often did in the spring [when Christians celebrated Jesus' resurrection, and the pagans in the popular Phrygian cult celebrated Attis' rebirth]... In some areas, interesting syncretisms appeared. The Roman Bishop Hippolytus, writing in the first half of the third century, described at length the cult of Naasenes, in which the worship of Attis and Jesus were thoroughly merged...Christian fathers found it necessary to pass canon laws against the practice of self-castration by fanatical ascetics in those very regions where the galli had once been so prominent..."[bc]

Julius Firmicus Maternus was a Roman Latin writer who became a Christian apologist during the reign of Constantine in the ancient Roman Empire when Christianity became legalized. Speaking of the "galli, priests of Cybele" and Attis in the mid-fourth century A.D., representing similar ecstatic practice and gender transgression, he wrote that:

"They wear effeminately nursed hair and dress in soft clothes. They can barely hold their heads up on their limp necks. Then, having made themselves alien to masculinity, swept up by playing flutes, they call their Goddess to fill them with an unholy spirit..."[bd]

The ancient church father Augustine also writes against this same spirit at work in the ancient Roman empire saying:

"Even till yesterday, with dripping hair and painted faces, with flowing limbs and feminine walk, they

passed through the streets and alleys of Carthage, exacting from merchants that by which they might shamefully live."[be]

Read plainly, gender confused men parading through the streets without shame in transgender drag expected compensation for their victimhood so that they would not have to work for a living but rather have their livelihood paid for by others.

Today, these same demonic forces are at work in the world and are seeking to seduce God's people into idolatry, syncretism, and apostasy. The demonic Ahab and Jezebel spirits can work in men or women but are particularly powerful when a male leader (including husbands) have the passive Ahab spirit and a close female leader (including wives) have the powerful Jezebel spirit. Today, these mighty demonic forces, along with others, are at work in everything from gender confusion to sexual sin, the gender mutilation and sexualizing of children, drag shows for the whole family, pornography addiction, sexual assault, Pride month, and abortion. The connection between sex and demonic spirits is a clear theme throughout the Bible. Commenting on the days of Moses in what sounds like a modern-day headline, 1 Corinthians 10:6-8 says, "These things have become examples for us so that we won't desire what is evil, as they did. So don't worship false gods as some of them did, as Scripture says, 'The people sat down to a feast which turned into an orgy.' We shouldn't sin sexually as some of them did. Twenty-three thousand of them died on one day."

What the Old Testament would call shrines, temples, and high places are now called strip clubs, porn sites, and abortion clinics. Cancel culture is nothing new, as the prophets who spoke out against these powerful demonic forces in the past were silenced, and the same thing continues in our day to any Bible preacher speaking light into the darkness as Elijah did.

The Jezebel spirit is always at work in the Church, politics, and culture, seeking to hold positions of power to put forth false teaching, encouraging gender confusion and sexual sin, as was the case in the church at Thyatira.[151] The church needs leaders like Elijah who will stand up against the Jezebel spirit to preserve the purity of God's people by calling them to repent of what they had previously been tolerating. Jezebel is always looking for passive Ahabs who will tolerate so she can dominate. In a church, an Ahab pastor, board member, staff member, or person in leadership is the equivalent of never shutting the front door on your home, as we will learn about next.

---

151 Revelation 2:20-21

28 Signs of the
Ahab Spirit

In one of the most horrifying scenes in American history, an 18-year-old gunman with no prior firearms experience entered Robb Elementary School in Uvalde, Texas to kill 19 students and two teachers.

Within minutes, police were on the scene carrying weapons and wearing body armor. Yet, they did not enter the school or do anything to try and stop the active shooter. In fact, no one entered the school or took action for over an hour while innocent adults and children were being slaughtered. In total, 376 law enforcement officers were on the scene—a force larger than the one that defended the Alamo—and stood passively by doing nothing. As distraught fathers descended on the school carrying side arms, law enforcement stopped the fathers from trying to save lives, even though the police were doing nothing!

The world was dumfounded at how this could possibly happen. It makes no sense, unless you consider that an Ahab spirit of passivity overtook the entire hellish scene, which allowed a controlling Jezebel spirit to rule a school and ruin lives.

The Bible Tells Us What Always Happens

The Bible tells us not only what happened, but what always happens. This is because the Bible is not an old book, but rather a timeless book, which means it is always timely. All the pains, problems, and perils in our world can only be understood by embracing Genesis 3 as the truest of truth.

Tragically, we read that Adam stood by silently while all the coup attempts on earth occurred; he failed to lead his family in godliness as Genesis 3:6 recalls, "...she [Eve] also gave some to her husband [Adam] who was with her, and he ate." Eve's sin was *commission*—she did what was forbidden; Adam's sin was *omission*—he did nothing to stop it.

This demonic pattern continues. Satan attacks marriage and family while passive, silent, non-relational, inactive men say and do nothing. God then came looking for the man first, holding him firstly responsible for the sinful condition of his family as its head. The pattern is crucial: though Eve sinned first, God held Adam firstly responsible because he was the singular head of his family. Genesis 3:9 says, "...the Lord God called to the man and said to him, 'Where are you?'"

At work behind the scenes of Adam and Eve, as well as Ahab and Jezebel, was Satan. He had previously declared war in Heaven, which was tolerated by the angels who became demons, but not tolerated by God, or His holy and loyal angels. Revelation 12:7-10 says:

> *"Now war arose in heaven, Michael and his angels fighting against the dragon. And the dragon and his angels fought back, but he was defeated, and there was no longer any place for them in heaven. And the great dragon was thrown down, that ancient serpent, who is called the devil and Satan, the deceiver of the whole world—he was thrown down to the earth, and his angels were thrown down with him. And I heard a loud voice in heaven, saying, 'Now the salvation*

and the power and the kingdom of our God and the
authority of his Christ have come, for the accuser of
our brothers has been thrown down, who accuses
them day and the night before our God.'"

Satan and his demons (including Jezebel and Ahab), continued their war against God, seeking to assert themselves as the singular head over all of humanity. Adam was passive, tolerating the satanic evil in his family, which opened the door for the demonic to overtake not only his family, but all that was under his dominion. The story of Adam and Satan is merely the beginning, a tragic pattern followed by king Ahab and the Satanic Jezebel spirit.

Demonic Possession, Oppression, and Tendencies

In studying the life and ministry of Elijah according to the Scriptures, including his battles with Ahab and Jezebel, along with their demonic spirits, we will now examine how these same spirits operate in our own day. The goal is to be discerning and able to "see the distinction between the righteous and the wicked, between one who serves God and one who does not serve him".[152] To be discerning, we must soberly and earnestly examine ourselves, as well as others, as there are three levels of Ahab and Jezebel influence.

One, some people are possessed by the Ahab and/or Jezebel spirit. They may even be clinically diagnosed with multiple personalities (i.e., dissociative identity disorder), which sometimes includes demons, whereas other times it is a mental or physical

---

152 Malachi 3:18

causation, but not spiritual. This was the case with the ancient queen Jezebel, as well as the woman acting like a prophetess in the church at Thyatira.[153] They have courage, resiliency, power, and confidence that has not only deceived them, but helps them deceive others. Their identity, decision-making, view of reality, and emotional and mental outlooks are nearly entirely controlled by this spirit. The spirit is so strongly at work through them as a counterfeit of being Spirit-filled that it is hard to draw a line of differentiation between the human being and the demonic being. They commonly also hear a voice speaking to them in their mind, and as they yield in obedience to it, they become overtaken by that spirit in their personality and decision-making.

Two, some people are oppressed by the Ahab and/or Jezebel spirit externally. They struggle at times to not come under demonic influence. This happened to the great man of God, Elijah, who was so oppressed by the Jezebel spirit that he ran for his life in fear some one hundred miles, wandered off into the woods, and wanted to die. Others oppressed by the Jezebel or Ahab spirit are tempted by her to align with them. Sometimes, when you are talking with someone who has the Jezebel spirit, for example, your thinking becomes cloudy, you don't feel completely in control of yourself, and you find them pulling you to think like them, agree with them, or support them. This is demonic oppression.

Three, some people do not have the Ahab and/or Jezebel spirit as much as they have Jezebel tendencies or, a passive or controlling personality. Perhaps they grew up in a home with this spirit, were married to someone with this spirit, or were trained in an unhealthy church or ministry with this spirit, as was the case in the church at Thyatira. Such people have picked up bad

---

153 Revelation 2:20-21

habits, bad doctrine, religious traditions, and family curses that they need to consciously be aware of and battle against to walk in godliness with joy. In the days of Elijah, this was the case with a godly man named Obadiah (a different man than the one the book of the Bible is named after). Obadiah was a man of God,[154] who "feared the Lord greatly", saying, "I...have feared the Lord from my youth." While Elijah was public and active with his faith, Obadiah kept it private and passive. Obadiah hid one hundred godly prophets, feeding and saving them from being killed by Ahab and Jezebel, but did not reveal to the king or queen his faith or private ministry. Upon encountering Elijah, fear gripped Obadiah and he initially declined to do as Elijah instructed, unwilling to inform Ahab and Jezebel that the prophet Elijah was coming for a supernatural showdown. Obadiah worked in a governmental position and is an example of a godly man who feared the demonic king and queen. Although Obadiah does demonstrate some passivity, having moments of Ahab-like behavior, he is not a man like Ahab. Some otherwise good Bible teachers wrongly say, "Obadiah is a picture of the compromising believer, and his life is in direct contrast to that of Elijah. Elijah was serving the Lord publicly and without fear; Obadiah was serving Ahab (vv. 7–8) and trying to serve Jehovah secretly (vv. 3–4) ...When Elijah confronted Obadiah, the frightened servant did not trust the prophet. And note that Obadiah had to 'brag' about his secret service to impress Elijah with his devotion (v. 13). Alas, we have too many Obadiahs these days and not enough Elijahs!"[bf]

The truth is, Obadiah overcame his initial fear and passivity to risk death to serve God by obeying Elijah. Obadiah confronted Ahab and Jezebel, telling them that Elijah the prophet

---

154 1 Kings 18

was coming. Sometimes, godly people start with more passive tendencies and personalities but, out of love for the Lord, over-come their fears and move from cow-

There are two primary ways to sin.

ardice to courage. If we are honest, we all have Ahab moments where fear for our own well-being, as well as those we love, cause our first response to be one of avoidance and passivity. However, like Obadiah, we can respond in the Spirit, override our avoid-ance, and march forward in faith.

There are two primary ways to sin.

One is commission, where we do something which we should not do. Examples include telling a lie, slandering someone, or stealing something. In the Garden, Eve sinned through com-mission. She acted independently of God and her husband and ate the forbidden fruit. The Jezebel spirit sins through commission.

Two is omission where we do not do something we should do. Examples include not telling the truth to combat a lie, not defending the reputation of someone who is being wrongly slandered or covering for an employee when you know they are stealing from the company. In the garden, Adam sinned through omission. He said and did nothing while Satan replaced him as the head of his household. The Ahab spirit sins through omission.

Lastly, before we learn to discern the Ahab spirit, when you are dealing with the demonic, it can be completely exhausting. We see this when Elijah ran 100 miles away from Ahab and Jezebel, wandered into the wilderness, and laid down so exhausted from constantly fighting them that he wanted to die. 1 Kings 19:3-4 says, "Then he was afraid, and he arose and ran for his life and came to Beersheba, which belongs to Judah, and left his servant there. But he himself went a day's journey into the wilderness and came and sat down under a broom tree. And he asked that he might die, saying, "It is enough; now, O Lord, take away my life…"

Demons Wear You Down

Elijah is completely exhausted. However, we never see Ahab or Jezebel this worn out. Why?

In our book *Win Your War* that is free in digital format and includes a free sermon series, my wife Grace and I write:

> "The limitations we have are natural. As created beings with limited energy, we all reach the point where we have depleted ourselves and say things like, 'I'm out,' 'I need a break,' 'I cannot do any more,' 'I just need to sit down,' and 'I've got nothing left to give.'
>
> Sound familiar?
>
> Now, consider the different reality in which angels live. Angels do not share in the limits of our humanity. Instead they sing and serve 'day and night' (Revelation 4:8; 7:15…What is true of angels is also true of demons. Satan's nonstop attack on believers is 'day and night' (Revelation 12:10). Demons do not need a nap, a day off, food, water, or sleep because they do not get tired or sick.
>
> Do you see the problem for you? If you have human limits, and demonic spirits who attack you do not share those limits, how can you possibly win a war against that foe since 'we do not wrestle against flesh and blood, but against the rulers, against the

authorities, against the cosmic powers over this present darkness, against the spiritual forces of evil in the heavenly places' (Ephesians 6:12)?

To win your war, you cannot fight by your own natural power. A natural person cannot win a spiritual battle against a supernatural demon. No one ever defeated the demonic by his or her own strength. No matter how self- disciplined you are, how hard you try, or how tough you may be, eventually the supernatural always defeats the natural.

Sometimes evil people live by the power of demonic forces and have a superhuman energy level. They harass and hound you until you are overwhelmed, exhausted, and overtaken. Jesus delivered two 'demon-possessed men' who were 'so fierce that no one could pass that way' (Matthew 8:28-34). People took the long way around the region where these men lived. Two men controlled an entire region—until Jesus cast their demons out.

In Mark 5:1–20 Jesus encounters 'a man with an unclean spirit.' With demonic strength, 'no one could bind him anymore, not even with a chain, for he had often been bound with shackles and chains, but he wrenched the chains apart, and he broke the shackles in pieces. No one had the strength to subdue him. Night and day among the tombs and on the mountains he was always crying out and cutting himself with stones' (vv. 3–5).

You know you are dealing with a demonized person when they do evil, never grow weary, and force everyone else to work around them, avoid them, and live in fear of them. The only way that you can win your war against demonic power is by the supernatural power of God the Holy Spirit: '...be

strong in the Lord and in the strength of his might'
(Ephesians 6:10). Our strength comes from the
Lord's strength and not our own. The Christian life is
supernaturally lived 'in the Spirit' by God's power at
work for you, in you, and through you. The counterfeit
of being Spirit-filled is being demon-possessed. When
someone is filled with the unholy spirit, your only
defense is to be filled with the Holy Spirit."

Elijah is among the most courageous, powerful, and anointed people in the entire Bible. Even he was exhausted doing spiritual battle with demonic forces. This was not because he was in sin, but because he was human. James 5:17 (TLB) says, "Elijah was as completely human as we are..." If he was overwhelmed and exhausted by the demonic, you will find yourself experiencing the same struggle at times. In ministry, we've seen numerous pastors quit their role simply because a few people in the church with the Ahab and Jezebel spirits completely wore down the pastor and his family until they could no longer serve in ministry, leaving service of God altogether in order to survive. One Ahab can open the door to a legion of Jezebels and other demons in a church or ministry. One Jezebel can exhaust an entire leadership team in a church, ministry, or company like a war of attrition where the shelling continues day and night until physically, mentally, spiritually, and emotionally, the servants of God don't have any fight left in them. One Ahab or Jezebel in an extended family or friend group can burn everyone out to complete weariness. This is doubly true in the days of technology where Ahab and Jezebel have platforms, form unholy alliances like the 850 prophets of Baal and Asherah, and declare war on truth preachers like Elijah day and night. They seem to never break from the battle, which is all digital spiritual war in the unseen realm of the Internet with demons who understand the algorithms better than anyone.

Discerning the Ahab Spirit

The driving personality trait of someone with the Ahab spirit is passivity. These people seek to avoid responsibility, conflict, and pretty much anything difficult. Their hope is that someone else will take care of them. The root words from which we derive the word "passive" refer to allowing suffering, which is exactly what passive people, especially leaders, do. An etymology dictionary explains the root meaning of the word "passive" as deriving "from Old French *passif* 'suffering, undergoing hardship'...and directly from Latin *passivus* 'capable of feeling or suffering,' and...*pati* 'to suffer'".[bg]

Some people wrongly see passive leaders as kind people who never have conflict, raise their voice, or have others dislike them. Their passivity is actually evil and tolerates evil, which then usurps them as the leader and causes suffering for others. These people look loving, but they are among the most unloving. Being loving and nice are two very different things. To be nice to evil is incredibly unloving. Here are some things an Ahab loves:

1. **Fear**—In the days of Elijah, King Ahab who ruled in Israel was ruled by fear. He spent most of his days in the safe confines of the castle surrounded by soldiers. He lived in complete fear of his demonic wife Jezebel. We never see him disagree with her, stand up to her, or correct her on anything. An Ahab is a fearful person, easily controlled and pushed around because they suffer from "fear of man".[155] Sometimes professional help and medication

---

155 Proverbs 29:25

can help with fear and anxiety. Sometimes the problem is more physical than spiritual and requires medical attention. Sometimes fear and anxiety are at least, in part, spiritual. If a demonic spirit is behind the fear, then the answer to the problem is spiritual. 2 Timothy 1:7 (NKJV) says, "For God has not given us a spirit of fear, but of power and of love and of a sound mind." The Bible speaks on occasion of various demonic spirits of fear including Apollyon, which is the ruling demonic spirit of fear that is the counterfeit to the Holy Spirit and faith.[156] The way to deal with a demonic spirit of fear is to cast it out and replace it with the love of God. This is why replacing worry with worship, fear with faith, and panic with prayer drives out the spirit of fear. 1 John 4:18 says, "There is no fear in love, but perfect love casts out fear. For fear has to do with punishment, and whoever fears has not been perfected in love." Ahab did not have the Holy Spirit or faith, and so he lived by the controlling grip of the spirit of fear. Ahabs are fearful people. They don't have long-range thinking and make impulsive short-sighted decisions out of their fear of hurt, loss, rejection, or difficulty. Their fear leaves them passive, and easily controlled by domineering people, which is precisely the relationship between the fearful and passive Ahab and his controlling and domineering wife Jezebel.

An Ahab spirit loves feeling entitled.

2. **Entitlement** - An Ahab spirit loves feeling entitled. King Ahab lived a very entitled life. Despite ruling over God's nation of Israel, from King David's throne, doing nothing but demonic sin and rebellion, he felt entitled to live a lavish life with his every need provided through the tithe

---

156 Revelation 9:11

and taxes of people. When Naboth declined his offer to purchase a coveted piece of land, he lay in his bed sulking like a child because he felt entitled to anything he wanted and could not emotionally endure not getting whatever he wanted. Today, the Ahab spirit is driving an entire younger generation toward socialism and the entitled expectation that the government should take care of both their needs and their greeds, throwing fits, calling themselves victims, and even protesting if they do not get what they want.

3. **Victimhood** - An Ahab spirit loves interpreting all data to see themselves as a victim, and never a villain. When Elijah confronted Ahab, he called the prophet of God the "troubler".[157] In Ahab's eyes, he was basically perfect like Jesus, and all the problems in his life and Kingdom were because of Elijah's abuse and mistreatment. As we studied earlier, the original word for "troubler" is sometimes called serpent, which means that Ahab thought the man of God was the devil. An Ahab spirit has taken a dominant position in western culture. It seems like the goal of most everyone is to find a way they were a victim, excuse their sinful behavior, blame others for their life's struggles, and demand compensation because they feel entitled.

4. **Coddling** - An Ahab spirit loves being mothered. The relationship between the passive Ahab and his controlling wife, Jezebel, is more like a mother and son than a husband and wife. She flatters him, reminding him that he is a powerful king, and then usurps his authority to make decisions for the nation. She sleeps with him, cares for him while he acts like a baby even though he's a grown man, and when he is sulking in his bed refusing to eat because Naboth would not sell him land, she

---

157 1 Kings 18:17

comes in to rub his back and tell him in effect, "my poor boy, momma will take care of this." An Ahab often grows up in a household where they were over-mothered, and under-fathered. Today, there is a record number of single young adults living with a parent into their 20's and 30's. Most of these are able-bodied young men who grew up without a father and can't fathom not having their mother pay their bills, clean their clothes, cook their meals, and fight their battles. These kinds of men do not marry until later in life, when they meet a Jezebel who will pick up where their mother left off.

5. **Emotionalism** - An Ahab spirit loves emotionally manipulating others. Ahab is the King of Israel, commands an army, and rules a nation from a throne in a castle. He is also known to sulk, whine, throw fits, and act like a toddler who needs a nap. When he is emotional, it's emotional manipulation. Like a child that sits on the floor yelling with tears rolling down their face, people with the Ahab spirit have learned that if they are passive and emotional long enough, someone will come along and take care of them. Jezebel does this very thing, murdering Naboth and stealing his land so that Ahab would stop sulking.

6. **Flattery** - An Ahab spirit loves to be praised and flattered. The only flattering compliments given to Ahab in the Bible come from his controlling wife, Jezebel, who flatters him solely to manipulate him. As he lay on his bed staring at the wall and refusing to eat his dinner in a full-blown tantrum, his wife sat next to him on the bed and "Jezebel, his wife, said to him, Thou art of great authority, and thou governest well".[158] An easy way to control and manipulate an insecure and passive Ahab is to praise and flatter them.

---

158 1 Kings 21:7, WYC

7. **Perversion** - An Ahab spirit love sexual perversion.
   As we examined earlier, the ancient artifacts that
   archaeologists have uncovered that portray Jezebel
   show her nude, sexual, and pornographic. The ancient
   Jezebel was known to be both pretty and perverted.
   Revelation 2:20–22 says that the woman with the
   Jezebel spirit in the church at Thyatira was, "seducing…
   sexual immorality and [adultery]…" The onslaught of
   sexual sin celebrated as love and liberation is evidence
   of the ongoing seduction of Jezebel. A Jezebel spirit
   will sleep with a boss to get a promotion, sleep with a
   leader to destroy their family and reputation and uses
   sex to manipulate those they date and marry. Men dating
   or married to a female with the Jezebel spirit tolerate
   what she does outside of the bedroom because of how
   tantalizing she is in the bedroom. In very twisted marital
   relationships, this includes permitting one's spouse to
   commit all kinds of sexual sin, overlooking, endorsing,
   or even joining them as a form of the sexual Jezebel
   controlling the addicted Ahab.

An Ahab Spirit Seeks to Avoid…

As a passive person, someone with an Ahab spirit seeks to
avoid several things. In each of these examples, you can sense
the underlying sense of selfishness. When the Bible repeatedly
extols servanthood, and the perfect example of Jesus our Servant
King, we see the exact opposite in the Ahab spirit. Jesus is a
King who "came not to be served but to serve, and to give his life
as a ransom for many".[159] Ahab was a counterfeit king who came
to be served, and to take from the lives of many. The following
are some indicators of the possible presence of an Ahab spirit.

159 Mark 10:45

1. **Headship**—The doctrine of federal headship comes from the Latin word for covenant. A covenant is the Bible's language to explain a relationship that binds people together. We tend to think of ourselves solely and exclusively in categories as individuals, but we're not. God sees us as part of a collective, as families, and as groups. Each covenant has a head, and the head's responsibility is to make sure the people of the covenant are cared for, and the terms of the covenant are kept. Adam is the head of the human race, or the federal head, in the same way that Jesus is the head of the Church, and the husband is the head of the family. Safeguarding every covenant is a head, a leader responsible for the keeping of the covenant terms. The Bible repeatedly says that Jesus Christ is the capital-H covenant "Head".[160] Regarding the family, the Bible also repeatedly says that the husband is the little-h "head" of covenant marriage and family.[161] As King of Israel, Ahab was supposed to lead as human head of the nation as the Christ-like head, but he continually rejected his responsibilities as head, deferring to his wife and others to function as head. As the husband and father, he was supposed to lead his family lovingly and humbly as a Christ-like head, but at work and home, he refused to own his headship responsibilities, which opened the door for his demonic and controlling wife to rule and reign. Christ loves us and took our place to deal with our sins and lead us into a better future in His Kingdom as our Head. People, especially leaders and particularly men, with the Ahab spirit do not own their role and responsibility as head and instead let the least healthy people in their life, including their own broken wives, function as head with catastrophic and painful results for everyone involved. The bottom line of an Ahab is their unwillingness to be a

---

160 Colossians 1:18; 2:10, 19; Ephesians 1:10, 22; 4:15; 5:23

161 Genesis 2:18, cf. 1 Timothy 2:11–15; Genesis 5:2; 1 Corinthians 11:2–16; 14:33–34; Ephesians 5:21–33; Colossians 3:18; Titus 2:3–5; 1 Peter 3:1

good head taking responsibility, making decisions, and sacrificing for others.

2. **Conflict**—Ahab avoids conflict. There is no record in his entire life of ever having healthy and necessary conflict with his demon-possessed, murderous, lying wife. In a difficult season, rather than standing up, we read that he "lay down on his bed".[162] An Ahab in conflict is one who lays down rather than stands up. The only conflict Ahab has with Elijah is when Elijah tracked him down to confront him to his face. Today, someone with an Ahab spirit will avoid conflict at all costs. They often have profound fear of man issues[163] and know they cannot defend their choices in life, so they avoid accountability and healthy conflict. One of the reasons Ahabs tolerate Jezebels is simply the fact that they too want to be tolerated and never confronted with any criticism or conflict. If you do confront an Ahab to have healthy conflict, it will likely never go well. They will avoid the conflict, change the subject, shift the blame, make an excuse, tell you why they are the victim, or accuse you of being mean, unloving, cruel, and a domineering bully. In a marriage, an Ahab will stay late at work, pick up lots of hobbies, intentionally get a job that requires a lot of travel, keep their headphones on all day, have nights out with friends minus the spouse, and hide out in some corner of the home hoping to avoid conflict at all costs.

3. **Overt living**—Ahab is a covert not an overt person. He never comes clean and is caught by God and confronted by Elijah. With an Ahab, you can never be sure what they are thinking or doing. In this way, an Ahab is a lot like Judas. He was on Jesus' ministry leadership team, sitting in class for three years, learning the Bible, praying prayers, and even likely raising his hands in worship.

162 1 Kings 21:4

163 Proverbs 29:25

The entire time, he was also stealing from and plotting the murder of Jesus. No one really knew who Judas was, until his covert life became overt following the Last Supper. An Ahab is a lot like Judas. If you are married to this person and end up divorced, you will be shocked at who they truly were, what they were really doing, and will likely never know the whole story.

4. **Leading at home**—For generations, the men in Ahab's family were horrible husbands and fathers. Generation after generation lived wicked lives until God killed them. You would hope that after nothing but demons and death, Ahab would at least inquire of the prophet Elijah if there was not a better way to live a life and lead a family. Elijah promised God would kill him and his wife and kids, all of which came to pass after God's patience wore out. At no point did Ahab make any effort to lead his family away from judgment and destruction. Those with an Ahab spirit can slowly watch their family crater and still not have any sense of urgency to lead them away from danger.

5. **Learning** - Ahab has one of the most powerful men of God in the history of the world regularly in his presence. Elijah was so amazing that God kept him from dying, taking him to Heaven in a chariot. God sent fire from Heaven to consume the sacrifice at Mount Carmel and sent two more fire strikes from Heaven to kill 100 of Ahab's soldiers. At any time, Ahab could have humbled himself and asked some questions to learn from Elijah. He never does. Ahab only argues with Elijah. Thousands of years later, we've spent considerable time in this Bible study seeking to learn from Elijah. Imagine getting private meetings with him and never learning anything! Instead of learning from Elijah, Ahab repeatedly argued with him. The Ahab spirit is both weak and proud. The apparent weakness is a deception that covers for the pride. Ahabs

do not seek out wise counsel, or godly learning, even if they are surrounded with Spirit-filled people like Elijah. Elijah was such a giant that people thought that John the Baptizer, and even Jesus, were Elijah returned. Yet, Ahab learned nothing from this man of God.

6. **Healthy spirituality**—Ahab and Jezebel are very spiritual. They practice witchcraft, divination, fund demonic cultic ministry, and are surrounded by idols. In a word, they are very spiritual without the Holy Spirit. Sometimes, people with the Ahab spirit who are the most confusing and deceiving are very religious, and very spiritual, but do not manifest the fruit of the Spirit working in and through them. Like Ahab, all they manifest is the works of the flesh. This same demonic spirit is at work all over the world, from priests who abuse children, to pastors who sleep with congregants, and people who are on staff at churches leading secret double lives in the darkness.

7. **Leading at work**—At work, Ahab is never the leader. He holds the position of king, but it is his wife Jezebel who makes the decisions, leads the nation, and rules and reigns. At work, a person with the Jezebel spirit will attach themselves to a stronger leader who will carry them to success and prosperity. Like a barnacle attached to a boat, they stick to a successful person and go along for the ride. Jezebel was the boat; Ahab was the barnacle.

8. **Picking a church**—Ahab let his wife literally choose the religions of Israel, a nation that belonged to God. She planted all the pagan churches, hired the pagan priests, and ran the pagan schools training the demonic leaders in witchcraft and the occult. She picked the religion of the nation and family, deciding where Ahab and the kids would worship. Today, an Ahab will let the Jezebel in the relationship pick if they go to church, and if so,

where. Once the Jezebel is displeased with someone or something in the church, they will leave and pressure the Ahab to follow, which they often do.

9. **Joy**—Ahab is quite an emotional person. We see him fearful, hiding, yelling, crying, and sulking. The one thing we don't see from him is joy. He's simply not a joyful person. He's burdened, successful, rich, powerful, broken, and depressed, but never joyful. Because joy is the fruit of the Spirit, as evidenced in Jesus who "rejoiced in the Holy Spirit",[164] joy is the emotional state of a healthy believer. Because he does not have the Spirit, Ahab does not have joy. Ahabs are not emotionally healthy or joyful. This is why being around them is not life-giving or burden-lifting. These people are life-taking and burden-giving.

10. **Difficult decisions**—When there are difficult decisions to be made, Ahab defers. Over and over, his wife Jezebel steps up to make decisions in his place. When the time comes to decide whether to go to war, Ahab consults 400 false prophets who are paid to only tell him what he wants to hear. Polling 400 false prophets to decide is the height of insecurity and passivity. Whenever there is a difficult decision to make, Ahab passively defers the decision-making to someone else. This is often because then he won't have to assume responsibility for the outcome of the decision. If things go well, he can take credit for decisions made by his wife or false prophets. If things go poorly, he can blame them. When dealing with an Ahab, they are the least helpful when needed the most. Ahabs are prone to the paralysis of analysis— going back and forth with research, opinion polls, pro and con lists, vacillating between opinions, being swayed by others—unable to simply make a difficult decision and stick by it. In contrast, Elijah makes one difficult decision

---

164 Luke 10:21

after another because he knows the will of God, so he has courage and confidence, trusting the outcome to God, and seeking to live in obedience, albeit imperfectly as he's still human like the rest of us.

11. **Sacrifice**—Ahab was known as a brilliant military strategist who would never get his hands dirty or endanger his own life. Men like Ahab are often good strategists and tacticians at work and war, but they keep themselves hidden at a safe distance from danger. When Ahab's troops went to war, the coward did not dress up like the king he was, because he knew it would increase the odds of sacrificing his own life. In contrast, the godlier king Jehoshaphat wore his royal robes into battle, trusting God whether he lived or died. That king, like our King Jesus, was willing to sacrifice his life for the good of his people. King Ahab, on the other hand, would rather sacrifice his troops than sacrifice himself. Any person with the Ahab spirit is not sacrificial. Their priority is always protecting and preserving their life, not doing what is right in the sight of God or helpful for others. In God's providence, Ahab died a miserable, shameful death and serves as a warning to those, like him, headed to Hell that they need the sacrifice of Jesus and to learn to live sacrificial lives like Him. Elijah serves as our example of this; he sacrifices his wealth, health, privacy, and security, risking his own life, to sacrificially serve God and the good of the nation.

12. **Generosity**—One thing we never see Ahab do in his life is give. He does a lot of taking—including Naboth's field—but no giving. When you are dealing with an Ahab, it is a give-and-take relationship. You give. They take. If an Ahab gives you something, it is intended to deceive you about who they are, not give you an accurate depiction of who they are. If you find that someone you've known for a long time has the Ahab spirit and

you look back, don't be surprised to find that they ate
a lot more of your food than you did theirs, spent a lot
more of your money than you did theirs, and got a lot
more benefit out of their relationship with you than you
did with them. The opposite of a taker is a giver, and the
God of the Bible is a giver who gave us His only Son and
the gift of salvation. Elijah understands this generous
heart of God and gives his whole life and reputation in
service to God and God's people.

13. **Correction** - An Ahab spirit hates being confronted and
rebuked. Ahab was repeatedly confronted and rebuked
by Elijah the prophet, and he never received it well. On
one occasion, Elijah told him to his face, "I have not
troubled Israel, but you have, and your father's house,
because you have abandoned the commandments of
the LORD and followed the Baals."[165] Despite this honest
evaluation, Ahab did not repent. In fact, he never repents.
Even when the 850 prophets of Baal and Asherah were
defeated and destroyed by God on Mount Carmel, Ahab
did not repent of his life of sin. Those with an Ahab spirit
are not moved by confrontation and rebuke. Even when
it is obvious that they are in the wrong, they avoid the
conversation, remain silent, and talk about how they
are the real victim. They try to change the narrative in
their favor or shoot the messenger by blame shifting so
that someone else is responsible for their wrongdoing,
thereby making themselves the passive victim. In some
cases, they have been so babied and coddled their entire
life that they cannot conceive of themselves as anything
but a good person doing what is right. For an Ahab, all
correction is interpreted as rejection, which strikes at
their deepest insecurity and need to be needed.

14. **Caring**—Throughout the life story of Ahab, the only
time we see him emotional is when he's being selfish.

---

165 1 Kings 18:18

Disobeying God by marrying the demon-possessed
Gentile Jezebel, supporting her destruction of the
worship of God and promotion of demon worship, killing
the prophets, and opposing God's servant Elijah, the
only time he shows emotion is when he might suffer.
When he was denied a minor real estate deal, 1 Kings
21:4 (NKJV) reports, "Ahab went into his house sullen
and displeased because of the word which Naboth the
Jezreelite had spoken to him; for he had said, 'I will not
give you the inheritance of my fathers.' And he lay down
on his bed, and turned away his face, and would eat
no food." The only other time we see him caring about
anyone is, yet again, caring for himself. Ahab's response
to Elijah telling him that God would hold him responsible
for Jezebel's murder of Naboth was that he "he tore his
clothes and put sackcloth on his flesh and fasted and lay
in sackcloth and went about dejectedly."[166] Those with
the Ahab spirit are very caring people; the only problem
is the one and only person they seem to care about is
themselves.

15. **Dirty work**—Throughout the marriage of Ahab and
Jezebel, he is passive, and she is controlling and active.
Ahab uses Jezebel to do the dirty work he does not want
to do. She kills the prophets, closes the schools of the
prophets, murders Naboth, steals his land, and puts out
the death sentence on Elijah. Even though Jezebel does
the dirty work, God holds Ahab accountable because he
intentionally married and tolerated an evil woman, letting
her do whatever she wanted without caring, checking,
or stopping evil. Today, the reason someone with the
Ahab spirit allows someone with the Jezebel spirit in their
life is so they can use them by letting them do the dirty
work. This passivity is intentional and allows the passive

---

166 1 Kings 21:27

person to deny any moral responsibility if things go bad because they never get their hands dirty.

16. **Family**—As we have studied, Ahab came from a long line of godless men and women who defied God and did evil. The entire family was one big multi-generational cursed line. Despite God killing his forefathers and promising to kill him along with his wife and kids, Ahab never cared enough for his family to warn them or lead them toward God and away from destruction. His combination of utter selfishness and passivity results in his own son worshipping demons, including Baal. People with the Ahab spirit will use the members of their family when it benefits them. They will act irresponsibly and push their burden onto friends and family. However, they do not love their family members enough to lead them. Some will sit by and remain passive and silent even as their own spouse or children are self-destructing. Of course, when the eventual demise of a family member comes, the Ahab acts like a victim, becomes emotionally manipulative, and uses even tragedy to benefit themselves.

17. **Doing hard things**—Ahab is a soft guy living a soft life. He's not in the fight for his god on Mount Carmel— instead he sends the 850 false prophets. Even when he heads to battle, he changes his appearance, hiding the fact he's a king so that he does not have to be in the fight. Pretty much every time there is something hard to do, Ahab remains passive, the controlling Jezebel takes charge, and she starts giving orders for other people to do hard things for her husband. The only way to mature is to overcome hardship. Character is built through doing hard things. The reason Ahab is immature and lacks character is because of his lifelong refusal to do hard things. This is now a cultural crisis as younger generations, especially of men, are not in school, the

workforce, or able to even pass the minimal fitness requirements for military service. People with the Ahab spirit have become incredibly skilled at avoiding doing hard things, with some even joking about it as if it were an admirable skill.

18. **Rejection**—Throughout his life, Ahab continually manifests insecurity. He lives in a codependent marriage with a demon-possessed woman because he is too insecure to live without her. When his simple and unneeded real estate offer is rejected by Naboth, Ahab goes into a full-blown depression. Even a hint of rejection triggers his insecurity. Today, Ahabs are very insecure, need to be needed, want to be wanted, and loved to be loved. They cannot handle rejection, which leaves them open to codependent and even abusive relationships. This is precisely the marriage relationship Ahab had with Jezebel; she would domineer, control, use, and abuse him—even committing crimes such as murder—and he stuck with her and never stood up to her because he feared being rejected by her.

19. **Discomfort**—As a king, Ahab, like the men in his family who preceded him for generations, lived a lifestyle of absolute luxury. Unlike most men in his day, he was never required to get up early, go to work, sweat, and live paycheck-to-paycheck. From womb to tomb, he was pampered and spoiled. Passive, he sat around the palace all day waiting for others to take care of him as if he were a small helpless child. He avoided hard work, conflict, and responsibility because those things are uncomfortable. The Ahab spirit worships comfort. Like Ahab, those with the same spirit enjoy sleep, sex, food, and drink until they start to self-destruct through excess. Our culture of addiction and obesity are simply varsity attempts at Ahab living.

20. **Initiative**—Throughout his life, Ahab waited for life to happen, reacted to the decisions of others, and did not take initiative. He did not choose his career, as that was chosen by his dad. We don't know exactly how he met his wife Jezebel, but it would not be surprising if she and her father, who was the king of a godless nation, sought out the passive and weak Ahab knowing that Jezebel could dominate him, thereby allowing their controlling demonic family to rule two nations. Jezebel chose their family religion, bringing the worship of Baal and Asherah in full to Israel. Elijah initiated the various conflicts with Ahab, including the battle on Mount Carmel between Elijah the prophet and Jezebel's 850 prophets. When he lost the real estate deal with Naboth, he took no initiative, but his wife Jezebel leapt into action. When God said he, his wife, and their kids would die in judgment, he again initiated no change of course on their path to Hell. The Ahab spirit is not one to take initiative. They watch their life happen as a spectator, let others make decisions, and hope things work out.

21. **Reality**—In Ahab's mind, he was from a successful family ruling Israel for generations, was a successful man reigning as king, and was a successful husband and father who remained married and raised up his son to succeed him as king. In reality, his family was demonic and killed by God, he was demonic and killed by God, and the son who succeeded him was demonic and killed by God...along with his demonic wife. Furthermore, Ahab was likely completely set up and had no accurate view of reality. His entire life, he was controlled, ruled, and dominated by his wife Jezebel. If he was the head of Israel, she was the neck. He may have been on top of the organizational chart, but he was not in control. Jezebel's father was an evil king from another nation, and he

married off his daughter to the passive Ahab, likely
knowing that his family would then rule not one, but two
kingdoms as she was "Jezebel the daughter of Ethbaal
king of the Sidonians".[167] There is no record of Ahab's
power in Ethbaal's kingdom but Ethbaal's family, through
his daughter Jezebel, held all power in Israel. When
someone has an Ahab spirit, they think they are winning
when they are losing, think they are leading when they
are following, and think they are wonderful when they are
woeful. The Ahab spirit does not accurately see or live in
reality, which explains why they don't change.

Since Ahab and Jezebel worked together, and their demonic
spirits continue to do the same today, we will study Jezebel next.
His passivity led to her opportunity to seize control and do evil.
Like Adam who was passive, and Eve who took advantage of
her opportunity to take control, God holds them both accountable but the husband firstly accountable. For example, although
Jezebel kills Naboth, steals his land, and gives it to Ahab while
he had no idea what she was doing, God kills them both, starting
with the husband, because he is partly responsible for the sin of
his wife through his passivity.[168] We will learn more about her in
the next chapter.

167 1 Kings 16:31

168 1 Kings 21:17-24

29 Signs of the
Jezebel Spirit

Jezebel, the controlling and seducing queen opposing Elijah roughly 3,000 years ago was empowered by a demon that continues their work today through different people. Her name means "un-husbanded", and "Baal is my prince" which explains her fierce independence and dominance. A Jezebel is highly spiritual and highly seductive. A Jezebel, like Queen Jezebel, seeks to be at the side of the man in power as she did with King Ahab.

Over a thousand years after Elijah, Jesus rebuked a church for tolerating the Jezebel spirit. Revelation 2:20-21 says:

> *"...I [Jesus] have this against you, that you tolerate that woman Jezebel, who calls herself a prophetess and is teaching and seducing my servants to practice sexual immorality and to eat food sacrificed to idols. I gave her time to repent, but she refuses to repent of her sexual immorality..."*

Three thousand years after Elijah, the Jezebel spirit remains at work in our world. She's also making a lot of headlines.

Stormy Daniels, infamous for her career as a porn star for Wicked Entertainment, is at the center of a legal case against former President Donald Trump for their adultery. Her birth name is "Stephanie", which means royalty and refers to a queen. Her stage name "Stormy" is the nickname for Baal who is the Canaanite "storm god" worshipped by Jezebel. She has a triple goddess tattoo on her neck as a counterfeit trinity. She is a professional witch or medium who sometimes works with the demon "Lillith", a pagan myth about Adam's first evil and non-submissive wife who committed adultery with Satan producing evil offspring as a half human, half demonic counterfeit of Jesus Christ. She lives in a former witchcraft coven and "haunted house" with her Catholic partner. She conducts spells and clairvoyance at the Wicked Wednesday market in New Orleans and says, "From November 2020 to November 2021, I did 250 oracle readings". An oracle reading is a high-level witch using a double deck of tarot cards to consult with demons to answer questions. She hosts the reality show "Spooky Babes" where they search haunted houses for demons. All of this is public fact that she has stated in interviews with media outlets.[bh bi bj bk bl]

An excerpt from her interview with Olivia Nuzzi, an award winning reporter with New York Magazine says:

> *"Stormy Daniels saged the room and shuffled the oracle deck [two tarot card decks]..."*

The article goes on to explain she brought the oracle deck:

> *"to ask the guides for help to see more clearly...She was having trouble connecting to the realm of the spirits. She shuffled the deck again. There. Between her palms, the force field of energy swelled. She dealt the cards. As if by magic, the room shifted. My ears began to ring. Tension spread across my forehead. My eyes filled with tears. I looked across the table and met the dealer's gaze. She was crying too...I was bewildered by the wave of emotion that seemed to*

wash over both of us at once. Why did we cry?
'Because it's real,' she said. 'It's chaos and death and
destruction.'"[bm]

THE POWER TRIP | APR. 10, 2023

How Stormy Daniels Sees It Ending The long afterlife of a forgettable fling with a reality-television personality.

By Olivia Nuzzi, New York's Washington correspondent

Jezebel Wants to Rule Everyone, and Everything

Wanting to replace the real God as sovereign Lord over all, the highest authority, ruling and reigning without peer, the Jezebel spirit is a spirit of control. Because the Jezebel spirit is a demon without a body, it is neither male nor female, but can work in and through a male or female.

As a Bible preacher, in my many years of opposition from the spirit, I have seen it manifest more often in women than men. Often, trauma opens the door for a woman to be Jezebellian. Out of fear, she gravitates toward control and becomes domineering and overbearing, finding ways to get their way in everything from being a bully, to throwing a fit, or seduction. A Jezebel without deliverance and healing will cause damage to their own husband and children, and even transfer their generational curse to their grandchildren.

It is possible for a male to also be a Jezebel since the demonic spirit can work in and through either males or females. Men with the Jezebel spirit are frightening, domineering, controlling, overbearing, sexually demanding, and abusive. Women and children are never safe with a male Jezebel. A male Jezebel will use their strength to use and abuse women and children, often in demeaning and degrading ways. A highly public example of a male Jezebel is Andrew Tate, the well-known online influencer for young men. He was raised Christian, became an atheist, and has also claimed to be a Muslim. He's a self-proclaimed "misogynist" who uses his physical strength as a kick boxer to intimidate and dominate women and Ahab men. He was arrested for sex trafficking and forcing women he seduced into sexual slavery for online pornography, from which he pocketed all the proceeds.

I have seen much spiritual deliverance in people throughout my ministry, but sadly report that full deliverance from the Jezebel spirit is something I have rarely seen. Usually, it begins with rebellion against godly authority and God's Word, leads to gender confusion, apostasy, tolerating and celebrating sexual and gender sins, and eventually ends up in a complete denial of God in the form of deconstructing the faith, or some form of androgynous pagan pantheism or panentheism.

In a church, one Jezebel can wear out an entire leadership team. Throughout Jezebel's life, we see nothing but controversy, lies, conflict, oppression, threats, and even death. The Jezebel spirit is a seductive and sensual spirit and incites unhealthy and ungodly soul ties in churches and ministries that lead to sexual sin, especially adultery.

People with the Jezebel spirit, especially women who have suffered trauma or abuse that left them open to bitterness and the Jezebel spirit, have been greatly empowered by the Internet. There, they can bear false witness, slander, and harass godly people and leaders effortlessly and without impunity. Some have even turned this anti-ministry against mainly Bible-believing orthodox heterosexual male leaders into their crusade in the name of God. People who have never led in ministry and are not qualified by character, education, or the laying on of hands from godly, Spirit-filled leaders, will exercise demonic levels of authority. They will hold anyone and everyone on the earth that they dislike on trial before their judgment seat in the name of such nonsense as "accountability", "discernment", and "walking in the light"—things they curiously do not do themselves, which is often the case with hypocrites.

If anyone should point out anything they have said or done wrong, an immediate emotional response is sure to come. This can be emotional manipulation in the form of talking about how they feel hurt, judged, unloved, and victimized or it can be an escalation to a personal attack to ignore the issue and instead destroy the person who has found them out. This character assassination often includes anonymous sources like the "worthless men" Jezebel employed as false witnesses, murderous threats like Jezebel decreed over Elijah after the defeat of her 850 false prophets on Mount Carmel, and even weaponizing the Bible and abusing Scripture to cover their own sin while attacking a godly person as Jezebel did with Naboth.

Discerning the Jezebel Spirit

The following are some characteristics of the Jezebel spirit taken from the study of the life of Elijah in the Bible and his battle with the demonic King Ahab and his wife Jezebel, along with what has been my experience, now in my 27th year as a senior pastor preaching through books of the Bible. I've preached in some of the most liberal, anti-God, and dark cities of America's west coast, largely to people without a Christian background with deep roots in witchcraft, the occult, addiction, sexual abuse, gender confusion, and almost any and every sort of perversion. Here are the things that a Jezebel hates:

1. **Authority** - A Jezebel will try and override authority with manipulation or overthrow it with a coup. If a Jezebel cannot control a person in authority (like Jezebel did with Ahab), it will seek to crucify them (like Naboth) or cancel them (like Elijah).

2. **No** - A Jezebel hates being told no. This explains why we never see Ahab telling Jezebel no. She always gets what she wants. He fears her wrath if he says no, and so, out of fear, she controls him to always say yes. Often, you don't even know that you are dealing with a Jezebel until they are fired, demoted, told no, or corrected. At that point the murderous Jezebel spirit that was covert and hiding becomes overt and hideous. Proverbs 9:7-8 (NLT) perfectly says, "Anyone who corrects the wicked will get hurt. So don't bother correcting mockers; they will only hate you. But correct the wise, and they will love you."

3. **Losing** - When, by God's power, the lonely prophet Elijah defeated the 850 prophets of Baal and Asherah chosen and funded by Jezebel, she was furious. Her response was a vow to her demon "gods" that she would kill Elijah to avenge her very humiliating public defeat. When her husband Ahab lost a real estate negotiation with Naboth, she murdered the man and stole his land to avenge the loss and emerge as the triumphant victor in the negotiation. A person with the Jezebel spirit is often competitive in an unhealthy way and to an unhealthy

degree. They will cheat at business, marriage, and even ministry to get what they want. If they lose, they will do all they can to destroy whoever defeated them, avenge their loss, and prevail as victor.

4. **Rebuke** - A Jezebel spirit hates being rebuked and called to repentance. Throughout the story of Jezebel, we see her constantly doing evil of every sort and kind. Not once does she repent, show any sign of remorse, or even give the faint hint that she may have said or done anything wrong. Jezebel walks around thinking they are perfect, the counterfeit Jesus. If you point some sin out to a Jezebel, expect them to double down on their self-righteousness, explaining with great passion what a wonderful person they are, all they have given and sacrificed, how they have been a victim their entire life, and how you have abused them and harmed them by attacking them. If backed into a corner, a religious Jezebel with a bit of Bible teaching will pull your gun out of your holster and point it at you, calling you the one with the Jezebel spirit. If they say it first, there's a certain percentage of people who will believe them. Proverbs 18:17 (NLV) says, "He who tells his story first makes people think he is right, until the other comes to test him." Jezebel did this very thing, having Naboth the innocent man publicly declared guilty on the testimony of "worthless men" who lied saying, "Naboth cursed God and the king."[169]

5. **Grace** - A Jezebel hates forgiveness and grace...for others. If a Jezebel sins against you, they will demand forgiveness and grace, especially if they are religious. However, if you sin against a Jezebel, they will hold a grudge, choose bitterness, and seek vengeance. They weaponize being wronged to further excuse their lust for control. If you fail them, then they believe they

---

169 1 Kings 21:13

cannot trust you and must control you so that you cannot hurt them, or anyone else, as they become saviors and defenders for others by crucifying you. A religious Jezebel is very skilled in what Jesus called the plank-speck game. They will stress your minor failures, while overlooking their major errors. Religious Jezebels who weaponize the Bible will use it as binoculars to find all your sin, rather than a mirror to see their own. Their approach to the Bible is law for you and grace for me, which is an abusive and controlling relationship using the Bible not for forgiveness and grace, but self-righteousness and control.

6. **Men** - A Jezebel spirit hates men, and the godlier they are, the more she hates them. As we have established, a Jezebel spirit can work through and against a male or female. However, in the biblical story of Jezebel, we see the power of a woman with this spirit in attacking and hating men. Jezebel's hatred for the husband she did not respect but did despise is perhaps most on display when she forges his signature on legal government documents to murder the innocent man's land. She hated Naboth, the godly man, so much that she had him killed for not being godly, which not only took his life but reputation. She hated the prophets of God so much she had them killed and closed their schools so that other men of God could not learn the word of God. She hated Elijah most of all, because he was strong in the Spirit of God and stood against her more boldly than any other man. The Jezebel spirit hates men, and the godlier and more anointed a man is, the more this spirit hates them. Often, a person with a Jezebel spirit, including a man, has been hurt deeply, or even abused and traumatized by a powerful man in their life. This could be an abusive grandfather or older relative, evil father, abusive boyfriend or husband, or sexually harassing boss at

work. The brokenness can lead to bitterness if unforgiven and unhealed, which opens the door to demonic torment. In the book Win Your War I authored with my wife Grace that is free in digital format, we write:

"In the physical realm, different modes of transportation (e.g., an automobile or airplane) carry humans from one place to another. In the spiritual realm, various modes of transportation carry demonic persons. Bitterness, or unforgiveness, is a vehicle by which demonic forces travel into your life and relationships...Jesus' point[170] is that when you allow your hurt to turn into hate, you invite demonic torment into your life, causing it to feel like you are serving a jail sentence in a dark and despairing dungeon. The image of the jailer in Jesus' teaching is Satan and the demonic realm. Satan and his demons condemn you, haunt you, and torment you. They encourage you to respond to your hurt by hurting others and to your torment by tormenting others. God creates forgiveness, and Satan counterfeits it with bitterness...James [3:14-15] says that what bitter people are doing 'is not the wisdom that comes down from above, but is earthly, unspiritual, demonic'...The Holy Spirit through Paul speaks of the miracle of forgiveness: 'Be angry and do not sin; do not let the sun go down on your anger, and give no opportunity to the devil.'[171] Anger is not a sin, as God Himself gets angry, such as when Jesus made a whip and drove corrupt religious businessmen from the temple. Anger, however, can lead us to sin if we are not careful."

Often people with the Jezebel spirit (especially women), are bitter against a real harm done to them, but rather than forgiving and healing, they choose unforgiveness

---

170 Matthew 18:21-35

171 Ephesians 4:26-27

and demonic access. In our day, these women feel justified in overthrowing male domination (which is wrong) and replacing it with female domination (which is wrong). In the life of Jezebel, she attacks numerous men, but never one woman. If you find a woman today at war against one man after another, especially if this is her online "ministry" then you can be sure you are dealing with a wounded Jezebel that has been taken captive by the Enemy to do evil in the name of good. In Israel, Jezebel was surrounded by castrated men physically,[172] and her husband whom she castrated emotionally. The Jezebel spirit hates men and enjoys castrating them, so they are powerless, weak, and able to be controlled. This is why Jezebel women are fond of weak beta-males who are happily castrated and controlled in the name of being progressive, enlightened, and woke (an awakening to a demonic spirit including Jezebel), the counterfeit of being born again of the Holy Spirit.

7. **Truthfulness** - A Jezebel spirit hates being honest about any pain, brokenness, or trauma in their life. A Jezebel often has a very painful past that opened them up to living in the flesh, becoming bitter, and choosing to live in brokenness, which all opened demonic strongholds. The more you get to know a Jezebel, you often come to understand why they are the way they are, even though they are evil. Some Jezebels will be overly open and honest about trauma and pain in their life, often even announcing it to the world online. However, this is not a person in a healing process seeking to help others (even if that is what they say or even call their ministry), but instead a tactic to excuse their behavior, blame shift to their abuser, and cause others to have compassion for them. This compels everyone to tolerate them, which is exactly how a Jezebel weaponizes even their own pain

---

172 2 Kings 9:32

for control to cause more pain for others. It is a twisted, dark, despicable, and demonic cycle.

Signs of the Jezebel Spirit

The driving motive of a Jezebel is control. Often because they were wounded in the past, they are driven to exercise complete control over their present and future. Like the battle in Heaven where Satan tried to control even God, the Jezebel spirit will seek to control anyone and anything that tolerates them, thereby giving them the foothold they need to establish a stronghold from which to control. The following are some signs of a Jezebel spirit. A Jezebel spirit seeks to control…

1. **Relationships**—If you are friends with a Jezebel, they will want to control who you are friends with, and who you align with them as enemies against. Since a Jezebel is fiercely independent, they will pressure you to be dependent upon them, using your need for them as power to control you. This is the kind of relationship Jezebel had with her husband Ahab. She was fiercely independent, and because he was weak and passive, she used his need for her to control him. She also controlled their other relationships. A Jezebel parent will seek to control adult children in any way they possibly can. In the church, a Jezebel will seek out the weak, hurting, needy, immature, and new believers to "befriend" them as the mature and strong one, only to give them bad teaching and create a divisive faction in the form of an unholy alliance to control the church and its leader.

2. **Money**—Because money is a form of power, a Jezebel will use money to control others. At work, a Jezebel boss will use your paycheck to control you, getting you to align with them in conflicts, and/or doing things that

are unethical to maintain an income. If a Jezebel relative gives you a gift, there will be strings attached. They will control how you spend the money, demand later that you repay it, or expect something in return later that is probably ungodly, but you feel pressured to make happen because they have controlled you with money. In marriage, a Jezebel will so control the finances that their spouse is really not a partner in life, but a prisoner for life. In the church, a Jezebel will want to get close to the finances, as Judas did, know what the pastor makes, demand lots of financial information, and threaten to stop giving unless their demands are met.

3. **Governance**—Just like the ancient Jezebel was "queen", and the Jezebel in the church at Thyatira declared herself "a prophetess", these people love to govern. They love titles, positions of influence, being known, getting credit for success (including taking credit for the success of others), and will do all they can to get on the board of a company or church, leadership team at a ministry or organization, and get as close to the senior leader as possible, just as Jezebel did with King Ahab. In a church or ministry, these people will volunteer lots of time and energy to make themselves indispensable, and ultimately to climb the ladder of influence. If they have led or governed in another organization, they will quickly let you know how vital they can be to your organization if you just tolerate them and let them do what they want, which is often couched in religious terms as their "calling" or "ministry".

4. **Churches**—In Israel, Jezebel sought to control the Old Covenant church, closing the places where the God of the Bible was worshipped, killing the Bible-teaching prophets, and closing the schools of the prophets, which were the centers for Bible teaching in the land. She then

demanded that new gods be worshipped, starting with Baal and Asherah. Year later, the Jezebel spirit working through a woman in the church at Thyatira declared "herself a prophetess" whose "teaching" included "seducing...sexual immorality", "teaching" the "things of Satan".[173] In both the Old and New Covenant church, the Jezebel spirit continually tries to rule, reign, and ruin Christian churches and ministries. If tolerated in a church, this spirit will become powerful and influential, whether the person operating by its power holds any official leadership position or not. In a denomination, this spirit will pull all the churches south toward bad doctrine and compromised character as we witness continually with mainline Protestant denominational apostasy.

5. **Preaching**—Jezebel literally killed God's prophets, replaced them with her 850 paid false prophets and hunted Elijah, seeking to murder him. In the church at Thyatira, the Jezebel empowered prophetess[174] asserted herself as the preacher and teacher. Jezebels seek to preach or teach in any arena they can—from school classrooms to political speeches, and of course the church. A Jezebel spirit will do almost anything to teach publicly with authority. In a struggling church that cannot afford a pastor, they will volunteer to teach. If they can get themselves on the board to control what is taught, and who does the teaching, they become deadly. If a Jezebel cannot be a teaching authority in a church or ministry, they will find ways to undermine, discredit, and exhaust the person who does teach to hopefully remove them in hopes of replacing them. Often, this spiritual warfare tactic includes magnifying minor character flaws in a preacher or teacher, inviting others with the Jezebel spirit to bring complaints or even charges against the

---

173 Revelation 2:20,24

174 Revelation 2:18-28

teacher, and creating mounting pressure for them to either change their message or be removed from their position.

6. **Information**—Jezebel controlled her husband Ahab by controlling the flow of information. In the account of murdering Naboth to steal his land, Ahab had no idea that his wife was forging legal government documents, hiring "worthless men" to give false testimony. Jezebels maintain control by controlling information. They ask a lot of questions, probe for private details of people's lives, and collect any data and information they can, all in an effort to use information, and the flow of information, to benefit themselves and harm others. In the age of technology, a Jezebel will hack your email, secretly record your conversations, and behave covertly, not revealing anything but collecting any possible information and keeping it like a stack of bullets kept with evil intent, to be fired when needed.

7. **Access to the senior leader**—As queen, Jezebel would have had control over who had access to her husband, King Ahab. She could, at any time, act as the go-between with her passive husband and everyone else. Jezebels are adept at getting themselves into strategic positions where they determine who has access to the leader. In a family, a Jezebel makes it nearly impossible to have a direct relationship with other family members—you must go through them to have approval to speak freely with another family member. In a business or church, you need to go through the Jezebel to have access to the leader, and the Jezebel will use this trusted position to misrepresent the wishes of both parties, not allowing them to meet or speak directly but rather only through the Jezebel mediator.

8. **Conversation**—In the days of Elijah, Jezebel does much of the talking, redirects the conversation toward whatever she decides, and often gets the last word. These are all control tactics that work well, especially with her passive husband Ahab. A Jezebel will demand that you answer their questions, redirect a conversation in a direction you do not feel comfortable with, and dominate the conversation with a constant deluge of words. If married to an Ahab, the husband is lucky to every get a word in and if he tries to bring up a subject, the Jezebel quickly hijacks the conversation, changes the subject, overwhelms with words, and makes sure to get the last word.

9. **Platform**—In the days of Jezebel, the prophets of God had platforms to preach from at the places of worship and in the school of the prophets. To control the prophets, Jezebel controlled the platforms. She closed the worship locations and schools, then killed the prophets. Instead, she chose her own counterfeit prophets, opened counterfeit schools, and wanted her, and not God, to decide who was platformed. God gave Elijah a prophetic platform, and Jezebel kept trying to control his platform in everything from a public showdown with her false prophets, to murder attempts on the life of Elijah. Today, Jezebels try mightily to control platforms. The suppression and censorship of Bible-based beliefs on the Internet is simply a fact. I've experienced it grossly many times. Anywhere there is a platform (social media, news outlets, publishing houses, speaking engagements, political offices, pulpits, etc.), the Jezebels will attack godly teaching and teachers, seeking to have them cancelled and de-platformed. Jezebels also set up their own counterfeit platforms, often dedicated to nothing more than building their platform by attacking the platforms of others with

negative anti-Christ ministry that is an act of spiritual warfare against positive pro-Christ ministry.

10. **Narrative**—To control a narrative is an act of spiritual warfare. Jezebel successfully controls the narrative with Naboth. The godly man did nothing wrong, but the very public false narrative was that "'Naboth cursed God and the king.' So they took him outside the city and stoned him to death with stones."[175] None of this was true. The person who had dishonored the king and cursed God was Jezebel, not Naboth. In classic projection, she publicly accused him of the very thing she was guilty of to set the narrative. Today, Jezebels like to break a story, be the first to share juicy gossip, tell their side of a story, and twist any facts toward a perverted version of the facts, which is nothing more than lies that benefit themselves.

11. **Mob**—Jezebel had a professional paid mob of 850 prophets of Baal and Asherah. She would use this mob to influence and control the entire population of Israel. At the showdown on Mount Carmel, the entire point was to have a large crowd of people show up for the showdown, and the false prophets to turn them into an angry mob against Elijah and anyone else who would dare remain devoted to the Lord. In the New Testament, we see a demonic mob like this form against Paul in Ephesus that ended up turning into a riot.[176] Jezebels like to draw lots of attention, get emotions running high, appealing to fear and anger in a crowd, and then turn the mob against godly leaders and teaching. In the day of technology and the Internet, Jezebel is constantly at work forming mobs and inciting digital riots.

12. **Agenda**—Throughout the story of Elijah, we see Jezebel

---

175 2 Kings 21:13

176 Acts 19

constantly seeking to set the agenda for everyone, from God's prophets who were in hiding due to her death sentence, to the 850 false prophets who did what she said, to Ahab her passive husband who she thoroughly dominated. She set the agenda for Naboth by killing the man for not entering a real estate deal so she could get Ahab a plot of land he coveted, and attempted to even set the agenda for Elijah, demanding he obey her instead of God and causing him to flee for his life on multiple occasions. Setting the agenda for others is a form of control. Today, Jezebels want to set the agenda for your life, tell you what to do, boss you around, give you orders, and don't want you to find God's will, as their goal is simply to impose their will. All that a Jezebel needs is for you to be passive, like Ahab, or tolerate it like the church at Thyatira.

13. **Time**—Jezebel is about control, and one of the surest ways to control people is by setting deadlines and making threats and demands, all intended to control time. Jezebel set just such a deadline for the murder of Elijah saying, "So may the gods do to me and more also, if I do not make your life as the life of one of them by this time tomorrow."[177] Hearing this so traumatized Elijah that he traveled around 100 hundred miles, hid in the wilderness, and wanted to die because he was gripped by "fear". Today, Jezebels control people by controlling time. They will show up early to a meeting to throw you off guard. They will arrive late to disrupt a planned agenda. They will give deadlines to anyone who will tolerate being controlled. This is yet another form of control.

14. **Decisions**—Over and over, we see the passive Ahab deferring the decision-making to Jezebel. There is seemingly nothing that she will not insert herself into,

177 1 Kings 19:2

making demands and decisions without ever seeking the counsel of others, or even conferring with her husband. Controlling, a Jezebel spirit is highly independent. This is readily apparent in their decision-making.

15. **Environments**—While we see Elijah traveling through Israel, Jezebel remains at home in the safe confines of the castle. If you want to speak with or see her, you must come to her, on her terms, which is just another form of control. The same is true today. When dealing with a Jezebel, they will want to control your environment. You will need to meet at their office or home, at the time that works for them, with others present of their choosing. They will choose where they sit and where you sit. Their seat will be in a power position as they seek to control you and the conversation by controlling your environment, having you be in their environment on their terms under their control. There is even a growing trend called "Living Apart Together" where a married husband and wife live in different homes rather than living together. This is what happens when there is a Jezebel spirit in the marriage. Rather than being controlled, the spouse simply gets a second home so they can have their own environment. In other marriages, this explains why the couple sleeps in separate bedrooms, or the husband has a man cave where he can hide from his wife in an environment she still seeks to control but with less success.

16. **Leaders**—Jezebel controlled her husband, King Ahab, 850 prophets of Baal and Asherah, the servants in her kingdom, and the citizens of Israel who were afraid of her. She even tried to control Elijah the prophet. A Jezebel is always trying to control the person in leadership, and if they cannot control them, they want to remove and replace them. Often, this is done by

the Jezebel taking a minor character flaw in a leader, magnifying it into something disqualifying, inviting anyone and everyone to give their false testimony like the "worthless men", and building a case to either reduce their power, or ideally remove them from power. In this way, the Jezebel spirit has a great fondness for the internet where people who have never met can be introduced by their demons who already know one another and love to make introductions.

17. **Family**—The families of Ahab and Jezebel had been evil and demonic rulers over kingdoms for generation. One generation after the next was raised to continue the demonic pattern of generational family curses. As we established earlier in this book, Jezebel's father Ethbaal's name means "with Baal" and he served as a priest for Asherah. Jezebel was born into a completely demonic family under a generational curse. Her son was killed by God for also worshipping Baal.[178] The incredible demonic power wielded by Jezebel is because, for generations, her family had worshipped demons and done evil. A family under demonic generational curses grows more evil and more adept at doing evil generation after generation as the counterfeit to the blessings that God bestows on families who walk in the Spirit for generations. A Jezebel will even weaponize their own children and grandchildren for control. They commonly pit family members against one another into factions, threaten to kick family members out of the family or will unless their controlling demands are met, and will weaponize everything from family gatherings to marriages, holidays, and funerals as opportunities to increase their level of control over others. If you are in a family business working with a Jezebel relative, their level of control and manipulation is multiplied as was

178 2 Kings 1

Jezebel's ruling over their family business as King and Queen of Israel.

18. **Gifts**—In the story of Jezebel, we see that she uses gifts to control her husband. A beautiful and seductive woman, sleeping with her had to come with some perks so long as he let her be in control, which kept her happy. In fact, a Jezebel is often not a very happy person, unless they are in control, because being in control is the one thing that makes them happy. Jezebel also got her husband Naboth's field as a gift, something he desperately wanted. A Jezebel will give you something you really want, even if it's something God forbids, so that they can control you. If you keep one of these gifts in your home or office, it often comes with demonic oppression and the reason the Jezebel gave it to you was to remind you of them, even when they are not present, which is yet another form of control.

19. **Image**—Jezebel was known for her image. She was a beautiful and sensual woman, and when she wanted to be seen by others, she did her best to put forth her best impression. 2 Kings 9:30 says, "...Jezebel...painted her eyes and adorned her head and looked out of the window." Today, Jezebels are often fond of the internet, especially social media. There, they lie about who they are by only posting a carefully crafted fake life that can include their perfect marriage, amazing children, spotless house, fun hobbies, and lavish possessions and trips, along with Bible verses and doing ministry to help those who are less mature and successful.

20. **Energy**—Because demons do not share in the limits of our humanity, a person with the Jezebel spirit will wear normal people out with a seemingly endless supply of energy. This very thing happens to Elijah as he is laying in the wilderness so exhausted that he passes

out, wanting to die, and needing God to supernaturally help him recover with a 40-day sabbatical to get his life energy back. A battle with a Jezebel is a war of attrition. They grind you down and wear you out. You will wonder if they have a job, ever sleep, or do anything in their life other than cause you pain and harm.

21. **Sexuality**—In the days of Queen Jezebel, people traded their freedom for the sexual pleasure she provided. The same was true in the church at Thyatira in Revelation where Jesus rebukes, "Jezebel...[for] seducing my servants to practice sexual immorality..." As we studied earlier in this book, the word Jesus uses for sexual immorality is the same root word from which the same English words "pornography" and "pornographic" are derived from. The Jezebel spirt works through sexual pleasure, and even perversion of any sort or kind. The overt perversion in all western culture, including the sex education curriculum for even young children in public schools, is confirmation of the Jezebel spirit's complete stronghold on every aspect of culture, starting with the Internet and pornography.

22. **God**—By outlawing the worship of God in Israel, tearing down the churches, closing the Bible teaching schools, and murdering the true prophets while replacing all of this with demonic counterfeits dedicated to Baal and Asherah, Jezebel was literally trying to control who the God/god of Israel would be. Furthermore, she tried to control Elijah, God's prophet, seeking to replace God as the head in authority over the man of God. Of course, a Jezebel cannot control God, but it does not mean they won't try. Like Jezebel, the Jezebels will bring syncretism into a church, ministry, or Christian family. They will tolerate sin, especially sexual sin. They will even assert themselves as teachers, preachers, and prophets, as happened with the Jezebel at the church in Thyatira.

As a warning, everyone manifests at least some traits like Ahab and Jezebel at various points. This is because we do not live constantly in the Spirit, and in our moments, we yield to our sinful flesh, and we present the worst version of ourselves. If you think you may have an Ahab or Jezebel spirit in your own life, you should prayerfully and carefully choose a godly Christian counselor who integrates the latest in counseling wisdom with Spirit-led prayer and Bible study.

As we head into the future, the Bible is clear that our world is getting darker and more demonic as we head into the last days. We will examine this next as we evaluate the state of current culture, government, and the Church as all are being oppressed by the woke folk who want to possess them.

14 Birth Pains in the Last Days Before Elijah and Jesus' Second Coming

When my wife Grace got pregnant with our first child, it was a series of events I will never forget. In the first weeks of the pregnancy, things were relatively normal and other than a bit of fatigue and nausea, Grace looked and felt like her normal self. A few months into the pregnancy, she had more symptoms including a baby bump, heartburn, aches and pains, and some restless nights trying to sleep. The closer we got to the birth of our daughter, the pains got more intense and frequent every day. In the final days and hours leading up the birth, things got really intense.

As I watched my wife's pain increase the closer we got to the birth, I was worried she was going to pass out, or even die. The entire ordeal was agonizing and overwhelming. It was difficult to see my best friend with painful contractions until, finally, we got to hold our little girl. In a birth, the worst pain is used to bring new life.

Birth Pains

Jesus says that the Last Days leading up His Second Coming will be a lot like the birth of a child, saying in Matthew 24:8, "All these are but the beginning of the birth pains." To repeat what we learned in the introduction to this book, as I worked through the life of Elijah, the words of Jesus from this verse kept echoing in my mind. In context, Jesus is talking about the signs of the end of the age, what the world will be like as we get closer to the persecution of God's people and increase of evil before the Second Coming of Jesus Christ. In this section of Scripture, Jesus foretells the destruction of the Temple, which happened in 70 A.D., which would be followed by false christs that were counterfeit anti-Christs; the increase of political conflict and wars led by evil rulers of godless nations; and physical and natural disasters referred to as "famines" and "earthquakes". Following all this, Jesus prophesied the outlawing of Christian faith, tribulation, martyrdom, increasing hatred of believers, and mass apostasy as numerous people fall away from the faith. Everything Jesus prophesied occurred in the days of Elijah in the nation of Israel under the demonic rule of King Ahab and Queen Jezebel. Today, everything Jesus promised is also happening as the birth pains intensify as the end of days approaches.

In the days of Elijah, we read of the increasing birth pains in 1 Kings 16. The report of one evil king who was then succeeded by an even more evil king reports the birth pains with more intensity and frequency of evil until Elijah entered the scene. First, we are told about a king who God rebuked for "provoking me to anger with their sins" (16:2). The next king, "made Israel to sin, provoking the Lord God of Israel to anger with their idols" (16:13). The next king was judged by God as his "house...burned...over him with fire and [he] died, because of his sins that he committed, doing evil in the sight of the Lord" (16:18-19). Next, the successor king, "did what was evil in the sight of the Lord, and did more evil than all who were before him" (16:25). These birth pains grew with intensity and frequency, which set the stage for the coming of Elijah as Ahab and Jezebel, "did evil in the sight of the Lord, more than all who were before him...[and] did more to provoke the Lord, the God of Israel, to anger than all the kings of Israel who were before him" (16:30,33). Then, Elijah entered the scene.

As we have studied, Elijah was eventually taken to Heaven before he died, and He will return.[179] Just as Jesus will have a Second Coming, so too will Elijah as he comes to prepare the way for Jesus, just as John the Baptizer did preparing the world for Jesus' First Coming in "the spirit and power of Elijah".[180] Revelation reports that Elijah will boldly preach repentance, be killed so that he finally tastes death, and then be resurrected to return to Heaven. Then, Jesus returns to save humanity from complete extinction as the birth pains culminate with the birth of complete newness of life with the curse lifted, dead raised, unbelieving sentenced to Hell, and the believing rewarded in Heaven. In the closing of the Old Testament, Malachi 4:5 predicts all this saying, "I will send you Elijah the prophet before the great and awesome day of the Lord comes."

Curiously, to this day the Jewish people anticipate the Second Coming of Elijah to prepare the way for Messiah every Passover Seder. They drink wine from five cups, not unlike the cup of Christian communion, with the final cup being the "cup of Elijah". This cup is placed on the table that, in faith, Elijah will one day return, and then the Messiah (Jesus Christ) will arrive to establish the Kingdom of God forever. Until that day, we are to wait in faith. As part of the celebration, Jewish children even open the door to check if Elijah has yet returned. Sadly, many Jewish people do not rightly understand that, just as the Scriptures foreshadow the first and second coming of Elijah, so too they foretell of the first and second coming of Jesus Christ the Messiah. Although Jesus was Jewish, along with most of

179 Revelation 11:3,6-13

180 Luke 1:17

the first Christians, sadly many Jews have missed Jesus because they confuse His first coming in humility to die and rise for us and His second coming in glory to rise us from death. Indeed, Elijah is coming again, and preparing the way for Jesus to also come again.

Throughout history, there have been the same birth pains in every generation. Like physical birth pains, these spiritual birth pains become more frequent and intense, Jesus intervenes before the complete destruction of all humanity by a combination of demonic forces working through corrupt leaders in politics, religion, and business just as in the days of Elijah. Mark 13:20 says, "if the Lord had not cut short the days, no human being would be saved. But for the sake of the elect, whom he chose, he shortened the days."

These birth pains have always existed since sin entered the world and will continue until Jesus removes sin from the world. For example, the birth pains intensified around Jesus' First Coming and the days of the New Testament and early Church under the reign of the demonic Roman King Nero (37-68 AD). Sounding like a male Jezebel, he slept with his mother, kicked his pregnant wife and their child to death, had a transgender same sex marriage with a man he had castrated and dressed up as a drag queen bride so they could consummate their wedding in front of their guests, and organized orgies that lasted for days while persecuting and martyring Christians.

Ahab, Jezebel, and the Woke Folk

In every age, you see the same demons working through new people bringing the same birth pains with greater frequency and intensity. Today, the passive Ahab spirit that creates weak, castrated, and passive men has largely abandoned the rule of every aspect of western culture to what is commonly known as Wokeism.

In a conversation with Nicodemus, Jesus said that people needed to be born, or awakened, again by the Holy Spirit. The demonic counterfeit of being born again is becoming "woke" by an unholy spirit. To be woke is to be uniquely able to see invisible forces of injustice, oppression, and victimhood everywhere in history and present culture. To quote an old Christian hymn, to become woke is to declare, "I was blind, now I see".

Woke folk believe that anyone who disagrees with their view of the world's pains, problems, and perils are blind to the bias, prejudice, systemic oppression, microaggressions, and various other ways most everyone is oppressed. Being woke means to see abuses by everyone in power, and the victimization of those who have historically been outside of power (e.g., ethnic, sexual, and spiritual minorities along with women and transgender people). They also believe in intersectionality—the more minority groups a person is a member of, the more oppression they have faced, and the greater victims they are. Furthermore, as a victim, they are not morally responsible for decisions that negatively impact their life or others, but rather are only victims that deserve compensation in the forms of wealth and power. For example, a young, ethnic minority, transgender woman who feels like a man trapped in a woman's body that is discouraged from undergoing gender mutilation is seen as the ultimate victim because their life intersects with multiple points of oppression and injustice which makes them a candidate for varsity level victim status.

To accommodate the oppressed victim, we are pressured to let them define reality for themselves and support whatever they deem best for their life. While this may sound loving, it often leads to allowing people to do harm to themselves or living with mental health issues that are celebrated rather than treated. For example, as mentioned earlier, a friend pastors a church where

Cancelling is the counterfeit of Jesus' crucifixion.

some of the Christian parents removed their children from the local public high school because a young woman, who identified as a cat, demanded that a litter box, which she used in front of other students, be placed in the girls' restroom. This was her identity and her "reality" and, as a rare outlier minority, to deny her this right was deemed oppressive and victimizing. These kinds of truly insane stories are proliferating with no end or wisdom in sight.

Anyone who disagrees with this woke version of "righteousness" by intersectionality is canceled for being unloving, intolerant, and hateful. Cancelling is the counterfeit of Jesus' crucifixion and cancelling happens everywhere from social media platforms to losing your job, or from being kicked out of the classroom for disagreeing with your teacher or being ostracized for not wanting to see biological males competing in women's sports or showering in women's locker rooms. Those people who are more awakened, enlightened, evolved, compassionate, and tolerant become the defenders of the Jezebel spirit and demand that everyone they face act like Ahab. Those Ahab-like people then choose passivity and tolerance to avoid the kind of murderous spirit the prophet Elijah stared down daily. If you stand up for truth and God like Elijah did, expect a mob to form like the 850 false prophets of Baal and Asherah.

The prevalence and power of the counterfeit of wokeism should not surprise us. In my book *Christian Theology vs Critical Theory*, which is free in digital format I say:

*"Around the 2010's the few hundred-year-old
term 'social justice' was picked up to serve as an
overarching category to describe hidden biases
and systematic errors across most every academic
discipline. The result was that social justice
'scholarship' pulled all disciplines under Critical
Theory making it the leading counterfeit metanarrative
to the gospel of Jesus Christ in the Western world.
Underlying Critical Theory is social Marxism.
Economic Marxism based upon atheism has so
fully proven to promise Heaven but only deliver hell
wherever it has been imposed, that it is an unsellable
option to most anyone who has enough life to fog a
mirror. Examples include the former Soviet Union,
China, Cambodia, Cuba and elsewhere where the
body count, killed by their own government in the
name of cultural progress, stacked up to nearly 100
million citizens during the 20th century alone. Cultural
Marxism has the same goals as economic Marxism
but, rather than kicking in the front door to rob a
home, it picks the lock and sneaks in the back door
to accomplish the same task of redistributing wealth
and power, when it actually only redistributes poverty
and powerlessness. All of this is done in the name
of justice, which is appealing to the Christian, since
you will find that same word in the Bible, albeit with a
different meaning. Just like the cults, note that words
are used from the Bible and completely redefined
so that the meaning is changed. Yes, the father of
lies has a thesaurus and PR firm. The subtle shift
from economic to cultural Marxism was moving the
focus from capitalists and workers to race, class, and
gender categories of oppressors, and the oppressed
needing violent revolution in the name of justice,
and the redistribution of power and wealth. It goes*

by many names, but you should pay attention when you hear things like 'equity' instead of equality, which is something altogether different, 'justice' or 'social justice', along with appeals to 'inclusion' which has little room for heterosexual Christianity, 'diversity' and 'tolerance' which are not diverse or tolerant enough to include Bible thumpers, and 'culturally responsive teaching' which are codewords for the intolerista. We tend to think of a cult or religion as being overtly religious with some concept of divinity relating to humanity. Even some atheists wary of Critical Theory have called it a 'new religion'. When combined with Christian apostasy, it becomes a cult. Critical Theory is a secular cult seeking to make Heaven on earth without God, and social justice without any cosmic justice, which is what Jesus accomplished for us through His death for our sins on the cross. For the Christian, our hope is the lifting of the curse, the raising of the dead, and the rule of King Jesus over all Creation forever. For Critical Theory, the hope is the lifting of the curse through social justice, which is accomplished by cursing and crucifying anyone and anything that disagrees with the demonic spirit of the Critic at work behind the scenes. Instead of resurrection, the hope is reconstruction through the redistribution of wealth and power via the government in the place of God, which is a demonic counterfeit and nothing new..."

14 Birth Pains in the Last Days Before Elijah and Jesus' Second Coming

As the birth pains increase in frequency and intensity before the Second Coming of Elijah and Jesus, the following are 14 specific birth pains that preceded Elijah's first coming in the days of Elijah and will precede Elijah's return as the Ahab and Jezebel spirits, along with Satan and the other demons. Human history will be a repeat of the battle on Mount Carmel, with a showdown between Elijah and the false prophets and the appearance of the following 14 preceding birth pains will make the end of days.

1. **Christs:** The Bible tells us that, in every age, there is the presence of a demonic antichrist at work in the world.[181] Jesus says these birth pains will increase toward the end of days saying, "For false christs and false prophets will arise and perform great signs and wonders... so will be the coming of the Son of Man.".[182] One Bible dictionary says, "The term 'antichrist' could mean either 'against Christ' or 'in place of Christ.'"[bn] Satan and every demon working for him as an antichrist seeks both to remove Jesus Christ and replace Him as ultimate authority. This war started in Heaven and continues every day on earth since Satan and demons dethroned Adam and Eve as rulers on earth. The demonic spirits, including Ahab and Jezebel who tried to remove and replace the real God in Heaven and Israel, continue to work through human leaders in business, politics, culture, and religion to rule and reign over everyone and everything everywhere. Apostate woke Christianity assists this deception with a counterfeit Ahab christ who is a passive, tolerant, weak, and castrated version of the real Christ that opens the door to gender confusion, sexual sin, and controlling unhealthy women ruling through the Jezebel spirit.

2. **Cowards:** Another birth pain leading to the Second Coming of Elijah and Jesus is the increased rule of Ahabs in politics and the church. Weak, passive, permissive leaders will promote tolerance of sin instead

---

181 1 John 2:18, 2:22, 4:3; 2 John 1:7

182 Matthew 24:24,27

of repentance of sin as their counterfeit gospel. This is the anti-gospel preached by the antichrists. In politics, this will lead to the adoration and adulation of male politicians who are ineffective empty suits with hollow souls, controlled by the Jezebel spirit in a repeat of the horrors in ancient Israel. In the church, some denominations and networks will be increasingly led by mere figureheads, powerless like the false prophets of Baal and Asherah at the showdown on Mount Carmel, lacking any evidence of the power of the Spirit, going through ridiculous religious routines and rituals. Examples would include transgender bishops in long flowing robes and churches flying rainbow flags because they have come out of Satan's closet. In evanjellyfish churches lacking spiritual vertebrae, the sole attribute of God they cling to is "love", which is weaponized to support same-sex marriage and force people to sing to God about freedom in Christ through a mask only after they have agreed to get a vaccine, registered for church, and stood six feet apart. The most likely place to find the cowards in the church is among the creatives. Entire worship and creative departments are run by woke apostates who have accepted Ahab into their head and Jezebel into their heart. If you don't believe me, look up the "Christian" artists you sing songs by on social media and see who they follow, what they like, and how they virtue signal their approval of the progressive parade to peril. There are some creatives remaining who have not bowed their knee to Baal, but the trend is troubling.

3. **Control:** The Ahab spirit will fight for nothing, and Jezebel will control everything. The Jezebel spirit seeks to seduce every aspect of culture with the perennially popular four horsemen of horror - money, fame, power, and pleasure. Jezebel will not rest until she rules over every aspect of culture. After overtaking colleges, she has now moved into every aspect of education

(especially sex, gender, sexuality, authority, history, and justice) including high schools and even the youngest students who are encouraged to discover their sexual preference and innate bias before they can even read full paragraphs. Unless there is push back, like Elijah did, Jezebel will never stop itself and must be stopped. This is why Jesus tells us in Revelation that tolerance is treason.

4. **Corruption:** Dictionary.com defines corruption as, "the act of corrupting or state of being corrupt", and "moral perversion; depravity", or "perversion of integrity." One birth pain in every day that increases until the last days is sexual corruption of every kind, as we have studied in depth throughout this book. It is hard to imagine that the "Bible" for mental health, the American Psychiatric Association's Diagnostic and Statistical Manual of Mental Disorders listed homosexuality as a mental disorder up until it's 1974 edition. In my lifetime, homosexuality has gone from a mental disorder to a civil right with an entire evangelistic Pride month proselytizing planet earth and seeking to convert anyone and everyone to the religion of sex that now has its' own denominations (LGBTQIA are each a denomination in the religion of sex). With marriage no longer defined as a man or a woman, the next mangling of marriage will be polygamy, which I am certain will be legalized in my lifetime. Eventually, it is likely that the age of consent for sex with a minor will be lowered because corruption has no conscience and Jezebel has never blushed.

5. **Castration:** Just as Jezebel was surrounded by her castrated male eunuchs, which we have studied in detail, so too in the last days the castration of both men and women will increase. Sex trauma, confusion, addiction, and perversion will become so common that mutilating God-designed genitalia will be the new counterfeit of

Jesus' broken body and shed blood as the sacrament for the Jezebel spirit sex. Even children will be encouraged to be castrated in this pro-death movement, making an irreversible decision that will change their life and end their legacy. Rather than repenting of their sin, generations under the deceptive delusion of the Jezebel spirit will conclude that God sinned against them, creating them the wrong sex, and repenting of God's sin against them with a knife to recreate what God "created wrong".

6.   **Children:** Ahabs and Jezebels love sex but not children. Throughout the story of Elijah, we learn nothing about any of their kids until they die, and their godless demonic son is reported to be just as evil. There are no encouraging scenes of family vacations, warm dinner conversations, or happy family holidays. The ancient worship of Baal and other demonic false gods in Israel included the sacrifice of children, "Archaeological work also has revealed that at least some Phoenician cults practiced child sacrifice in accordance with what is noted in the Bible (2 Kings 16:3; Jer 7:31; 19:5–6)".[bo] In my book Abort Abortion, which is free in digital format I say:

> *"When sex is a demonic religion, dead children are the sacrifice. The sacrifice of one's child is the demonic counterfeit of the death of the Son of God for our sins. This demonic activity is nothing new and is common throughout the Old Testament." I go on to explain that even during the peak years of COVID-19, with the most inflated and inaccurate statistics, the leading cause of death was still abortion. While the world shut down for a supposed pandemic, the most dangerous place to be was not in a church with unmasked and unvaccinated people singing to Jesus, but in your own mother's womb. If a child does live, parents with the passive*

Ahab spirit send their children to a government-run school that is ruled by Jezebel who indoctrinates rather than educates the child. The goal is always the same—confuse, sexualize, and corrupt the child with sexual sickness, addiction, and mental health.

7. **Curriculum:** Just like Jezebel in the days of Elijah, the Jezebel spirit wars against Christian education, closing schools and killing or running off Bible teachers, thereby making it nearly impossible to have God's Word be the educational centerpiece even for God's people because of state overreach. Bible-based schools that dare to remain open can expect to be starved to death financially, harassed continually, mocked on social media, and litigated into misery and poverty, all in the name of loving tolerance and diversity. Mobs will descend on Bible teaching churches and schools, just like the 850 false prophets of Baal and Asherah did in the days of Elijah. This birth pain will only increase with intensity as the Second Coming of Elijah and Jesus approach.

8. **Closed:** As we learned in 1 Kings, Jezebel closed all the public worship of God in Israel. Remarkably, she closed every church and forced the remnant of remaining believers to meet underground illegally, thanks to the leadership of Obadiah that preserved a remnant of worship in Israel. When you see churches closed, and worship of the real God illegal, then you know that Jezebel is running the government and Ahab is running the church.

9. **Compromise:** As we have learned, in a war with Jezebel, she deceives Ahab-minded religious leaders to wrongly believe that syncretism and apostasy are a compromise where both sides win. In any war with a Jezebel, if she wins, then God loses. If Jezebel cannot close the church,

she will compromise the church. This was on full display in the days of Elijah, as we have studied. Jezebel allowed people to worship God in name only, so long as they also worshipped Baal and Asherah with sinful sex and golden calves. Today, the woke mob with cancel culture has filled many religious leaders with the spirit of Ahab. Scared of being sued, criticized, kicked off social media, or run out of the pulpit, Ahabs are ruling church boards, serving on church staffs, and preaching soft, scared, timid, tender, meaningless messages from the pulpit that are as helpful as a Nerf gun in a live round military firefight. Elijah would be kicked off most church boards, never make it through most Bible colleges or seminaries, would have zero chance of getting elected to run a Christian denomination or network, be banned from social media, and have woke beta males speaking out against him online to build their base and pay their bills while they stay home at a safe distance from anything that looked like picking up a cross.

10. **Confusion:** In the days of Elijah, the Ahab and Jezebel spirits controlled generations of God's people in Israel. They suffered under a strong delusion, not unlike being hypnotized under the power of a deceiving spirit. In 2 Thessalonians 2:8-12 (NIV), Paul says of the Last Days birth pains that precede the Second Coming of Elijah the Tishbite and Jesus the Christ, "The coming of the lawless one will be in accordance with how Satan works. He will use all sorts of displays of power through signs and wonders that serve the lie, and all the ways that wickedness deceives those who are perishing. They perish because they refused to love the truth and so be saved. For this reason, God sends them a powerful delusion so that they will believe the lie and so that all will be condemned who have not believed the truth but have delighted in wickedness." In a day when many Christian churches and denominations are supporting

gender dysphoria even in young children, encouraging ecumenical prayer with members of other religions, and backing politicians who claim to be Christian but are running on the platform of supporting abortion up through live birth (which is murder to any sane person with a modicum of a functioning conscience), the words "powerful delusion" are the only way to make sense of the world in which we live.

11. **Counterfeits:** In the days of Elijah, there were innumerable counterfeits. God's Kingdom was and is ruled by the Father, Son, and Holy Spirit. Israel was ruled by Satan, Ahab, and Jezebel. God's prophets were led by the men Obadiah and Elijah. The counterfeit prophets were led by the demons Baal and Asherah. The Old Testament Church was replaced with counterfeit shrines, temples, and high places. God's truth was repeatedly countered with Satan's lies. From top to bottom, everything God created Satan counterfeited in the days of Elijah. This same deception continues in our day as we have studied in everything from false prophets to false apostles, teachers, spirits, and doctrines. Just as a new cult formed in the days of Elijah when the worship of the real God was syncretized with pagan and occultic belief, so too it will be that new cults will appear (not unlike Mormons and Jehovah's Witnesses in the past) as we approach the end of days. In the name of "tolerance" and "social justice", expect them to blend things like supernatural mysticism and witchcraft (which is seeking to control God and the spirit realm); ancient paganism in the form of a worship of the earth as sacred; preference for God as Mother instead of Father; a radical commitment to transgenderism; the eradication of leadership and law; hatred of male leadership in the home and church, saying it's only toxic; and sexual anarchy and child sacrifice. All this mixed together turns into a new and powerful cult that is defined by who and

what it is against rather Who and What it is for. The anti-Christ spirit will create an anti-Christian cult. If this sounds familiar, it's because former "Christians" who are now apostate and known as the "deconstructionists" have started reconstructing the outline for what is emerging as an informal cult without a visible human leader but is instead ruled by invisible divine leaders thanks to the convening power of technology and demons. I have been battling this spirit my entire life, and it started as the Emerging Church, and today goes by names such as "Red Letter Christians", "Progressive Christianity", and other names with the first words always being a version of "anti", as behind it all is the spirit of antichrist.

12. **Cancelling:** In the days of Elijah, the prophets of God were cancelled. Some were killed, others were silenced and driven into hiding, and their platforms were taken away (e.g., their churches were closed, as were their schools). The prophets of God were no longer allowed to publicly speak God's truth. They were outlawed, banned, forbidden, throttled, and de-platformed. The only exception was Elijah, who refused to be cancelled and kept preaching, even challenging the 850 false prophets of Baal and Asherah to a very public battle between God and the gods. The counterfeit of Jesus' cross is cancel culture. In cancel culture, the woke mob sits in Jesus' judgment seat and decides who they will nail up for saying or doing anything that brings them to wrath. In cancel culture, someone's reputation, career, platform, income, and future are beaten, flogged, and crucified before a jeering mob (often online), to then be buried but never resurrected. Behind all of this is the Accuser who brings condemnation that leads to death rather than conviction that leads to life. Like the omniscience of God, in the age of technology, anything you have ever

said or done is brought forth for your public sentencing before an angry mob like Jesus and Paul faced. False accusations are also brought forth by false witnesses, and, in the name of justice, you are publicly scorned, attacked, maligned, and scourged by people who see what they are doing as righteous because they are deceived by the Deceiver. Even minor flaws or errors, including humor, style or tone are magnified online by the woke mob of "victims" triggered by curiously everyone but people who agree with them. As an aside, once someone is a public figure, the libel and slander laws do not apply to them in the same way that they would be a private citizen. This explains why a politician or celebrity can be beaten like a piñata with no recourse, but if the same thing were done to their landscaper, it would be a crime. The point? Be very wary of believing what the cancel culture mob is saying—especially if it is about a public figure who believes the Bible. The Father of Lies knows this well and uses it all the time to crucify leaders with cancel culture, especially as we approach the end of days when even Elijah will finally be cancelled and killed. Until that day, anyone who speaks the truth will get occasionally worn out as Elijah did, needing 40 days of recovery to battle his spiritual depression as we have studied in this book. Pray for those who speak the truth like Elijah. They are going to endure a lot of beatings on their way to blessings.

13. **Conflict:** In the days of Elijah's first coming, the birth pains increased in frequency and intensity until everything culminated with the final showdown between God and Satan, light and darkness, truth and the lies, Heaven and Hell on Mount Carmel. As we approach the Second Coming of Elijah and Jesus Christ, it will feel like this world cannot continue for much longer. Like a mother nearing the birth of her child, the bleeding,

screaming, and hurting will be intense. Then, Elijah will return to announce the final showdown at the end of days. They will cancel Elijah by killing him, but God will raise him to vindicate him, and one day has the same plan for you. Then, Jesus Christ will come down with fire from Heaven for the War to end all wars. Until that day, the birth pains will increase until Jesus defeats the demonic and the Kingdom of God rules over all Kings and Kingdoms, replacing the Ahabs and Jezebels with the children of God who will rule and reign forever in their place.

14. **Courage:** Until the conflict is won once and for all by Christ, if you are a believer in Jesus, you are called to take a stand in these dark days as Elijah did in his day and will do in the last days. Like the prophets with Obadiah who remained faithful to the Lord like Elijah, no matter how dark the demonic days become, there is always a remnant. Paul speaks of the birth pains leading up to the end of days saying in Romans 11:1–6, "I ask, then, has God rejected his people? By no means! For I myself am an Israelite, a descendant of Abraham, a member of the tribe of Benjamin. God has not rejected his people whom he foreknew. Do you not know what the Scripture says of Elijah, how he appeals to God against Israel? 'Lord, they have killed your prophets, they have demolished your altars, and I alone am left, and they seek my life.' But what is God's reply to him? 'I have kept for myself seven thousand men who have not bowed the knee to Baal.' So too at the present time there is a remnant, chosen by grace. But if it is by grace, it is no longer on the basis of works; otherwise grace would no longer be grace." In my book Theology For Everybody, which is a 365-day devotional on Romans free in digital format I say of Elijah:

"The prophet feels desperate and alone, like many Christians feel in today's world. God responds by correcting Elijah: 'Yet I will leave seven thousand in Israel, all the knees that have not bowed to Baal, and every mouth that has not kissed him'...God has a remnant of 7,000 faithful believers. God's people are everywhere. There may not be a lot of them, but there are enough of them. Whether in a church, a denomination, a city, or a nation, there is always a remnant God has reserved. God sees you, and He can bring you together with other believers to encourage each other mutually and partner together for ministry. This is what Paul is talking about in Romans 11, and out of it comes remnant theology. Now, as with many theological expressions, there is a bad version of remnant theology. Sometimes small ministries or churches are self-righteous; they see themselves as 'the remnant,' but then they judge others and don't have a heart for lost people. They have a suspicion of any place God is moving and working, and they accuse people there of compromising the truth. A healthy remnant theology maintains that God always preserves a remnant and brings believers together so they can reach more people for Jesus. The goal is not to just be the remnant but to be the remnant that comes together for the cause of Christ."

Not only are the Ahab and Jezebel spirits at work with increasing power in the last days, so is the Holy Spirit. God is asking you to be part of the Elijah remnant, standing up for the Lord in a world that will seek to silence and stop you from speaking the truth. Please remember that on Mount Carmel, when Elijah stood alone, the people watched, and many were saved. I am sorry that the world and demons are against you, but God is in you and for you as He was Elijah, and people are watching you as they were Elijah. If you are part of the remnant then your greatest ministry comes from your greatest misery, your worst day is your best opportunity, and the battle you are in belongs to the Lord!

These are the days of Elijah! Will you stand like Elijah? To help you do just that, in the next chapter we will learn how to overcome the Ahab and Jezebel spirits at work in our world.

10

Overcoming the
Ahab and Jezebel Spirits

Theresa grew up in a very unhealthy home. For generations, the women in her family had been into witchcraft, the occult, and casting spells. For a few years when she was a child, her mother worked at an occultic bookstore that hosted covens for witches to gather. She spent her days there helping her mother and engaging in witchcraft.

On numerous occasions as a child, she was sexually abused in these rituals by men and women. In college, she got a degree in women's studies, and was a very liberal goth chick who had jet black hair, makeup, fingernails, and clothes. Very intelligent, she had a successful career in the corporate world and in various seasons of her twenties lived and slept with men and women as a bisexual.

In her late twenties, she met a Christian guy who was in a prodigal season not walking closely with the Lord. Growing up in a very conservative religious home, Jack found Theresa very interesting because he'd never met anyone like her. Jack had a very shy personality, was successful in his career, and very intelligent with numerous advanced degrees. Theresa became very aggressive early in their relationship, pursuing him in and out of the bedroom. As a more passive personality, he let her make the decisions for both of them, and she made his fantasies come true so long as he remained passive and obedient in their relationship. The one time he tried to stand up to her, she became enraged and he was scared of her, so he never did it again.

Eventually, Theresa proposed marriage to Jack, and they got married while drunk in Las Vegas. Within a few years, Theresa got pregnant, giving birth to their first child, which was a girl. Late one night, Jack noticed that Theresa was not in bed, so he went into the nursery assuming she would be there with their baby girl. His wife was asleep holding their daughter in a rocking chair...and the chair was rocking even though it was levitating a few feet off the ground!

Terrified, he blurted out "Theresa", which awoke his wife and daughter who remained in the chair that was suspended in the air. He asked her what was happening, and she said her mother and grandmother did the same thing when they rocked their daughters to sleep.

Jack knew the Bible well enough to realize this was all demonic, in his home, and in his wife and now being transferred generationally to his daughter. Jack realized his passivity had allowed demonic evil into his home and family, and he traded sexual pleasure for Satanic presence. Jack rededicated his life to Jesus Christ, returned to church, began praying over his home and family, and digging into the Bible to learn about the demonic. In a word, Jack got activated. Theresa was not happy about any of this. She screamed at him, threatened to leave him for another man, and for some months, life felt like an internship for hell.

Thankfully, she eventually renounced the evil in her life and generations of her family. She became a genuine Christian; everything from her appearance to her personality changed over time. I got to witness this change as her pastor and baptize her. She admits to still struggling with tendencies toward control and seduction but has been delivered from a multi-generational demonic stronghold that was Jezebellian.

3 Levels of Demonic Influence

As we learned earlier in this book, there are three levels of man-ifestation of Ahab and Jezebel tendencies.

One, some people are possessed, or often nearly entirely controlled, by the Ahab and/or Jezebel spirit. This was the case with the ancient queen Jezebel, as well as the woman acting like a prophetess in the church at Thyatira.[183] The spirit is so strongly at work through them as a counterfeit of being Spirit-filled that it is hard to draw a line of differentiation between the human being and the demonic being.

Two, some people are oppressed by the Ahab and/or Jezebel spirit externally. They struggle at times to not come under her influence. This happened to the great man of God, Elijah, who was so oppressed by the Jezebel spirit that he ran for his life in fear some one hundred miles, wandered off into the woods, and wanted to die. Others oppressed by the Jezebel spirit are tempted by her to align with her. Sometimes, for example, when you are talking with someone who has the Jezebel spirit, your thinking becomes cloudy, you don't feel completely in control of yourself, and you find them pulling you to think like them, agree with them, or support them. This is demonic oppression.

Three, some people do not have the Ahab and/or Jezebel spirit as much as they have Jezebel tendencies. Perhaps they grew up in a home with this spirit, were married to someone with this spirit, or were trained in an unhealthy church or ministry with this spirit, as was the case in the church at Thyatira. Such people have picked up bad habits, bad doctrine, religious traditions, and family curses that they need to consciously be aware of and battle against to walk in godliness with joy.

183 Revelation 2:20-21

When we live in the flesh instead of the spirit, we are all prone to at least manifest some Ahab and Jezebel tendencies. The line between the flesh and the demonic is a blurry one, as most people who live by demonic powers started by giving footholds that became strongholds by first living in their sinful flesh for a period of time. Like gravity that pulls things south, living in the flesh eventually pulls us down into the demonic.

In reading this book, and studying the corresponding Scriptures to learn from the lives of Ahab, Jezebel, and Elijah, we learn some practical action items we can implement in our own lives:

1. **Choose the Spirit over the flesh and demonic.** People live either by the power of the Spirit, their sinful flesh, or demonic powers. When dealing with an Ahab or Jezebel spirit, their demonic presence will greatly tempt you to respond in the flesh instead of the Spirit.[184] In those moments, if you succumb to your flesh, you will say and do things that give them what Paul calls footholds and strongholds. If you respond in the flesh, you are giving them a victory. If you respond in the flesh, repent of your sin, and still call them to do the same, you have turned your defeat into a victory for righteousness. Elijah won his battles with the flesh and demonic by the Spirit and we do the same.

2. **Confess any sin to God that has put a foothold in your life.** If you have been manifesting Ahab or Jezebel in possession, oppression, or tendencies, confess that to God as sin, own it, and repent of it. As God helps you recall specific examples, confess those specific sins.

3. **Forgive.** If you have been hurt by an Ahab or Jezebel, Satan wants to use that to encourage bitterness in you, which is a greater entry point for the demonic. When all

184 Galatians 5:16-26

is said and done, the only two cultures in eternity will be Heaven and Hell. Today, you stand between Heaven above and Hell below. If you choose bitterness, you will pull Hell and demonic oppression into your life. If you choose forgiveness, you will invite Heaven and the Holy Spirit down into your life.

4. **Do not give in to a spirit of fear.** When dealing with an Ahab, or especially a Jezebel, it is common to be tempted to give in to a "spirit of fear".[185] The spirit of fear works with other spirits, including Ahab and Jezebel, to cause people to not believe and behave in ways they know by the Holy Spirit are right and true. Often, this Spirit of fear manifests in the "fear of man",[186] where we do not do what God says because we fear what someone else will do. Elijah is a model example of a person who lived in faith, and admittedly struggled against but overcame the spirit of fear with God's help.[187]

Do not tolerate.

5. **Do not tolerate.** As we examined earlier in this book, the Jezebel spirit gains power by being tolerated. Both Ahab and Jezebel were unhealthy and ungodly, but they tolerated one another in a dysfunctional and demonic relationship. When you are dealing with an Ahab or Jezebel spirit, you cannot tolerate such things as lies, control, sin, or evil. Elijah serves as our example of not tolerating and instead confronting and standing against evil.

6. **Confront.** The one thing Elijah kept doing was confronting Jezebel and Ahab, along with others who

---

185 2 Timothy 1:7

186 Proverbs 29:25

187 1 Kings 19:3

were acting in overt sin. We must first confront the sin in our own lives to ensure we are not hypocrites, and welcome godly people to speak truth to us as well. Then, we can act as Elijah did, and confront what God calls us to so that we are not tolerating evil.

7. **Speak the truth in love.** There is always hope that an Ahab or Jezebel could repent and be transformed by the power of the Holy Spirit. When confronting an Ahab or Jezebel we must resist the evil working through them, while loving them. To be sure, people are not victims of the demonic, as most of the time the power they hand over to evil is done so through living in the sinful flesh. Jesus began His ministry reminding us that he came to give spiritual "liberty to the captives".[188] Our hope must be that the person comes to the Lord and comes to their senses, although that is between then and the Lord. Elijah was patient to speak to Ahab and Jezebel over and over, which was very loving, and they were sadly never listening.

8. **Be a peacemaker, not a peacekeeper.** A peacekeeper will do most anything to ensure there is not conflict or confrontation. On the other hand, a peacemaker is willing to have the hard discussions and work through the difficult issues to get to peace through a bit of a battle. Jesus is both the Prince of Peace and a Warrior. He will return to have a war, and after that will come peace. Elijah was constantly willing to have the conflict, in hopes that Ahab and Jezebel would come to repentance and have peace with God.

9. **Always have a witness.** In the life of Elijah, we see him having an assistant, and later Elisha traveling with him. Because you cannot trust an Ahab or Jezebel, you need to document any conversation, conflict, or contract. They

---

188 Luke 4:18

will use information as ammunition so it's wise to have a witness in any interaction.

10. **Maintain clear boundaries.** Elijah did not move in with Ahab or Jezebel, did not sit down to dine with them, and never took any money from them. He gave them no ability to eradicate healthy boundaries between their life, worship, and possessions and his. In contrast, for political peace, Jehoshaphat did not maintain clear boundaries, giving his son to marry the daughter of Ahab and Jezebel, which destroyed his legacy.

11. **Be willing to separate.** There came a day for Elijah when he had nothing more that the Lord was asking him to say or do, and so he moved on with his life. At some point, you may need to get a Christian counselor to meet with you and your spouse, hire an attorney to untangle a business deal, move away from toxic relatives, find a new church with Bible teaching in the context of healthy relationships, cut off the engagement, block someone on social media, change your phone number, or stop hanging out with that friend.

12. **Expect emotional manipulation and attack in response.** Ahab emotionally manipulated, often through sulking, tears, or begging. Jezebel emotionally manipulated, often through seduction, threatening, or lying. Elijah endured a lot of negative emotional manipulation, and you will need to do the same.

13. **Be patient to see if there is real change or just fakery.** Because Ahabs manipulate through passivity and Jezebels manipulate through control, you can forgive them quickly but must trust them slowly. Forgiveness is free, but trust is earned. If they show remorse, it may be worldly sorrow as we saw with Ahab. Time will tell, so give it time.

14. If the person suffering from possession or oppression of an Ahab or Jezebel spirit is someone you know, you need to try and get them help from an integrative Christian counselor who is filled with the Holy Spirit, knows the Scriptures, and understands the latest clinical insights on counseling, such as the emerging fields of trauma and brain science. In my ministry, I have had a lot of very painful encounters with women who are Jezebellian, and their husbands who are Ahabs. Often, the wife has had some very real and evil trauma in her past that she has not healed from. In everything from nursing bitterness to believing lies, and making inner vows, her life gets a little darker and bleaker every day. These kinds of couples often attend a church with an Elijah leader because they are intrigued by the strength. The Ahab finds the strength curious as Ahabs are weak, and Jezebels find the strength attractive and even a challenge to seduce sexually, or attack and discredit professionally. Often, the husband knows that his wife is unwell and tolerates her brokenness and unhealth because he feels sorry for the trauma and abuse she has suffered. However, it is not loving to allow someone to become the worst version of themselves and inflict pain on everyone close to them, starting with their own children and friends. The best thing to do is get professional help for yourself and the spouse or child you love before complete destruction occurs as the demonic never stops until it has brought death. If the demonic foothold in a family is not dealt with in one generation, it only multiplies in the next generation. Demonic footholds that are passed from generation to generation become strongholds. For example, Jezebel's daughter Athaliah controlled the one-year reign of her son as King of Israel.[189] When her son died in battle, she had all the potential male heirs to the throne killed so that she alone

---

189 2 Kings 8:27-28

could rule and reign for six years as the only queen ruling without a husband.[190] Jezebel's daughter was a stronger Jezebel than her mother and is the only woman in the history of the world to rule alone as queen over Israel.

Passive, Aggressive, and Assertive People

In counseling circles, there is a distinction between passive, aggressive, and assertive people. Passive people are like Ahab, aggressive people are like Jezebel, and assertive people are like Jesus and Elijah.[bp]

An assertive person is open and honest about what they feel, think, and want. Unlike the passive person, an assertive person is overt and communicates honestly. Unlike the aggressive person, they are not unkind, harsh, or domineering. Instead, they honor themselves and the people they are in relationship and communication with. They will express their desires, feelings, and thoughts in a way that invites other people to connect with them and builds their relationship in a healthy way. Assertive people are known by others but not controlling of others. Unlike a passive person who lacks confidence, or an aggressive person who has arrogance, an assertive person has a healthy and humble confidence. Unlike a passive person who is taken advantage of, and the aggressive person who is unwilling to compromise and must get their way, the assertive person stands up for their own rights but also makes concessions in consideration of others.

As sinners, we all start more passive like Ahab or controlling like Jezebel. Perhaps most of us are a combination of the two depending upon our season of life and who we are dealing with

---

190 2 Kings 11:1-3

or what circumstances we are faced with. The key to becoming an Elijah is ongoing repentance of our sin to be filled with the Holy Spirit as Elijah was. The one thing we never see Ahab or Jezebel doing, despite repeated rebukes and patient waiting from God through Elijah, is repentance of personal sin.

In evaluating yourself, and your relationships, it's important to seek wise counsel to help you discern who you are and how you relate. There are six kinds of relationships between Elijahs, Ahabs, and Jezebels:

1. **Ahab + Ahab = passive.** These people console one another but get taken advantage of by others.

2. **Ahab + Jezebel = abusive.** The Ahab tolerates to avoid conflict, and the Jezebel dominates. This was the marriage of the king and queen in Israel.

3. **Ahab + Elijah = conflict.** An Elijah will confront and rebuke an Ahab who does not change, which creates ongoing conflict as Ahab and Elijah had.

4. **Jezebel + Elijah = standoff.** Since Jezebel will not repent, and Elijah will not tolerate evil, these relationships end in a standoff until God intervenes as He did for Elijah.

5. **Jezebel + Jezebel = dangerous.** Two Jezebels who align are like two barrels on a gun and capable of great evil.

6. **Elijah + Elijah = godly.** Two Spirit-filled godly people have the kind of relationship that Elijah had with Elisha.

Of course, the goal of a Christian is to not just move away from being like Ahab or Jezebel but move toward being like Elijah who is like Christ. If we are becoming "conformed to the image of his Son" to quote Paul,[191] we will become less and less

191 Romans 8:29

like them and more like Him. The type of Christ present in the lives of Ahab and Jezebel is Elijah. He is the Spirit-filled man of God. Although he is imperfect, unlike Jesus Christ, he brings the presence, power, and prophecies of God to Ahab and Jezebel repeatedly.

In Biblical studies, a type is, "an element found in the OT prefigures one found in the NT...The initial one is called the 'type' and the fulfillment is designated the 'antetype.' Either type or antetype may be a person, thing, or event..."[bq]

In Jesus' day, some thought He was Elijah, "Jesus...asked his disciples, 'Who do people say that the Son of Man is?' And they said, 'Some say...Elijah...'"[192] The similarities were so numerous between Elijah and Jesus that some confused the two men. Elijah's name means, "My God is Yahweh", and Jesus Christ is Yahweh. Elijah[193] and Jesus[194] spoke prophecies. Elijah[195] and Jesus[196] multiplied food. Elijah[197] and Jesus[198] raised the dead. Elijah[199] and Jesus[200] controlled the weather. Evil kings tried to kill Elijah[201] and Jesus.[202] Elijah[203] and Jesus[204] fled from evil kings into the wilderness. Elijah[205] and Jesus[206] spent 40 days

---

192 Matthew 16:13–15; Mark 8:27-30; Luke 9:18-20

193 1 Kings 17:1; 2 Kings 1:1-4, 17

194 Matthew 24:3-51

195 1 Kings 17:14-16

196 Matthew 14:17, 15:34; Mark 6:38, 8:7; Luke 9:13-17; John 6:9

197 1 Kings 17:17-23

198 Matthew 9:18-25

199 1 Kings 18:41-45; 2 Kings 2:8

200 Matthew 8:23-37; Luke 8:23-24

201 1 Kings 19:2; 2 Kings 1

202 Matthew 2

203 1 Kings 19:1-4, 10

204 John 11:46-54

205 1 Kings 19:8

206 John 11:46-54

and 40 nights in solitude. Elijah[207] and Jesus[208] preached boldly against sin. Elijah[209] and Jesus[210] were taken up to Heaven while others looked on in amazement.

Elijah serves as our example of being a godly, healthy, and assertive person in a world filled with passive Ahabs and aggressive Jezebels. In Elijah, we see the fruit of the Spirit manifest, whereas in Ahab and Jezebel we see the works of the flesh.[211]

During His earthly life, Jesus (the greater Elijah) faced every temptation and every demon. What is often overlooked in the life of Jesus is His personal relationship with the Holy Spirit. Christians talk a lot about a personal relationship with Jesus, which is wonderful, but we cannot forget that Jesus had a personal relationship with the Holy Spirit. The only way to overcome temptations and demons, is to live by the same power that Jesus did. I wrote an entire book on this called *Spirit-Filled Jesus* and preached a sermon series on it as well (you can find both at RealFaith.com in the sections marked "sermons" and "store"). In summary, Jesus was born into a Spirit-filled family with His parents Joseph and Mary (exactly the opposite of Ahab and Jezebel); Jesus announced at the beginning of His ministry that "the Spirit of the Lord shall rest on Him"; He had the Holy Spirit fall on Him at His baptism; Jesus lived "filled with the Spirit"; He had his emotional life regulated as He "rejoiced in the Spirit"; Jesus defeated the devil "full of the Holy Spirit"; He had healthy relationships with people (wise, foolish, and evil) by the discerning power of the Holy Spirit; He did supernatural ministry like Elijah "in the power of the Spirit"; and upon going

---

207 1 Kings 21:17-24
208 Matthew 11:22-23
209 1 Kings 2:11
210 Acts 1:9-11
211 Galatians 5:16-26

up to Heaven like Elijah, Jesus sent the Spirit down to empower us to follow Him as Elijah did. This is the only way to discern and defeat any demonic spirit, including Ahab and Jezebel. If there is anything in your life that is inhibiting you from living in the fullness of surrender to the Holy Spirit because you are passive like Ahab, controlling like Jezebel, or tolerating like the church at Thyatira, you need to pray to God, confess your sin, cancel that foothold, and claim your authority in the Spirit!

Heavenly Father

I thank you that you have loved me, adopted me, forgiven me, and begun a process to make me more and more like Jesus Christ.

I confess that I have been passive, controlling, and tolerating. These are sins against you.

I cancel any foothold I have given my flesh or the demonic in my life and family. I confess the sins of my family, and any generational patterns or curses that I have continued rather than crucified.

I thank you that Jesus lived the perfect life I have not lived, died the death I should have died, and gives the gift I cannot earn. Jesus Christ, you are Lord over my life, and it all belongs to you.

Lord Jesus, thank you that when you died and rose for me, you took me from the Kingdom of darkness to your Kingdom of light. I thank you for taking me from being a child of the Devil to a child of the Father.

I claim my authority in Christ to live out of my new identity as a child of God, by the power of the Holy Spirit, to become like Jesus Christ to the glory of God the Father.

I pray against the Enemy, his servants, and their works and effects in my life and family.

I take back any ground I have surrendered to the Enemy in his spiritual war against me.

I invite the Holy Spirit to fill me, occupying every aspect of my being and life, empowering me to live in the victory won by my King, Jesus Christ!

In Jesus' name.

Amen

When Will Elijah
Return to Earth for
His End Times Ministry?

In the old western movies, it was common that the movie would end with the hero riding off into the sunset. This theme was so common that the idiom "ride off into the sunset" has become a well-known metaphor for a peaceful and restful future following a life lived battling against evil doers. In many westerns, the closing scene was the good guy wearing a white cowboy hat as he rode into the sunset. In this final scene of Elijah's earthly life, we do not know if he was wearing a white cowboy hat, but we do know that the Lord sent a horse for him to ride off into the sunset.[212]

God's prophets had been told by revelation that the time had come for their fearless leader, the mountain man Elijah, to be taken to Heaven without tasting death.[213] This had happened only once prior with Enoch. Genesis 5:24[214] says, "Enoch walked with God, and he was not, for God took him."

Like Spiritual Father, Like Spiritual Son

For the latter portion of his ministry, Elijah was blessed to have Elisha with him as a faithful friend and trustworthy assistant. The relationship between these men was like father and son. In fact, Elisha refers to him in this scene as "my father".

---

212 1 Kings 2

213 2 Kings 2

214 cf. Hebrews 11:5

We all have physical fathers. This is the man with whom we share a genetic physical connection and general longing to have a relationship with and loving help from. We also have spiritual fathers. These are Christian leaders whom we share a spiritual connection with. In addition to physical parents, the Bible teaches that we also have spiritual parents. This explains why we ought "not rebuke an older man but encourage him as you would a father" and to treat "older women as mothers". [215] Like Elijah, Paul was a spiritual father himself, even though there is no indication that he had any biological children: "For though you have countless guides in Christ, you do not have many fathers. For I became your father in Christ Jesus through the gospel". [216] Paul also refers to Timothy, Titus, and Onesimus as "sons" and calls the Christians in Galatia "my little children." This is the heart of spiritual fathering and the kind of relationship that Elijah had with Elisha.

Once Elijah is taken to Heaven, Elisha faithfully carries forth the message and mission of spiritual father. Today, in business or ministry leadership, we would call this succession. The insight is that the best successor to a godly leader is someone who sees the previous leader as their father and learns from them to continue their work in new ways.

Reminiscent of the days of Moses when God parted the Red Sea, God then performs yet another miracle as the prophets of God look on. It must have felt something like a sports team watching the greatest player to ever play the sport take his last shot, or a legendary soldier firing his last round before walking off the field of battle forever. In 2 Kings 2:8, we read of Elijah at the Jordan River in which Jesus would later be baptized, "Elijah

215   1 Timothy 5:1-2

216   1 Corinthians 4:15

took his cloak and rolled it up and struck the water, and the water was parted to the one side and to the other, till the two of them could go over on dry ground." Following Elijah's departure to Heaven, Elisha crosses back over the Jordan by striking the water with the cloak of Elijah, parting it yet again. It is evident that the anointing was transferred to the next generation of leadership.

In an emotional farewell scene where Elisha will say his last goodbye to Elijah, he makes one request in 1 Kings 2:9-10, "When they had crossed, Elijah said to Elisha, 'Ask what I shall do for you, before I am taken from you.' And Elisha said, 'Please let there be a double portion of your spirit on me.' And he said, 'You have asked a hard thing; yet, if you see me as I am being taken from you, it shall be so for you, but if you do not see me, it shall not be so.'" Elijah was empowered by the Holy Spirit. What Elisha is asking for is the same anointing. The anointing of the Holy Spirit is the power and presence of God to be at work for us, in us, through us, and around us. Elisha rightly knows that to continue supernatural ministry will require the Spirit of God.

In what is truly a first-class flight, God sends a chariot with horses to deliver Elijah home as he rides off into the sunset. For Elijah and the other prophets standing below, watching him fly away might have felt like a scene from a Christmas movie with flying reindeer transporting Santa Claus.

Throughout his life, Elijah honored God. As we have examined, he was not a perfect man, but he was a great "man of God." God honored Elijah with a very public homecoming unlike anyone before or since.

Elijah and Jesus

The reason Elijah battled ungodly kings on earth was because he was fighting for his God King in Heaven, Jesus Christ. Many years after Elijah went up, King Jesus came down. Jesus was empowered by the same Holy Spirit as Elijah, and the two men were so much alike that some thought Jesus was Elijah come back down to earth.[217]

On one occasion, Elijah did make a brief return trip to earth to a mount other than Carmel, what we now refer to as the Mount of Transfiguration. There, Jesus along with Peter, James, and John were visited by Moses and Elijah.[218] The inner circle of three disciples, along with the two great prophets, were present to see Jesus, who was living in humility, reveal Himself as God in glory.

It seems that Elijah will return to earth one last time to finish his ministry, preparing the way for Jesus' Second Coming. Malachi 4:5-6 says:

> *"Behold, I will send you Elijah the prophet before the*
> *great and awesome day of the Lord comes. And he*
> *will turn the hearts of fathers to their children and*
> *the hearts of children to their fathers, lest I come and*
> *strike the land with a decree of utter destruction."*

This prophecy has a double fulfilment because Jesus comes to earth not once, but twice.

In Jesus' first coming, this prophecy was fulfilled by John the Baptizer who prepared the way for Jesus' first coming. Numerous Scriptures reveal this fact.[219] The key is that John the

---

217 Matthew 16:13–15

218 Matthew 17:1–13, cf. Mark 9:2-13; Luke 9:28-36

219 Matthew 11:11–15, 17:10–13; Mark 6:14–16; Luke 1:16–17; John 1:19–23

Baptizer came, "in the spirit and power of Elijah",[220] as he had the same Holy Spirit anointing as was given to Elisha. When asked, "'Are you Elijah?' He [John] said, 'I am not.' 'Are you the Prophet?' And he answered, 'No.'"[221] The similarities between Elijah and John the Baptizer are many. One, both men have a similar prophetic gifting and ministry.[222] Two, both men dressed in eccentric mountain man ways.[223] Three, they both lived in the wilderness.[224] Four, both men preached repentance of sin. Five, both men had battles with evil kings and queens.[225]

Elijah's Second Coming

In Jesus' second coming, the prophecy of Malachi will be completed and fulfilled by Elijah. Prophesying the time leading up to Jesus' Second Coming, Revelation 11:3,6-13 says:

> "'...I will grant authority to my two witnesses, and they will prophesy for 1,260 days, clothed in sackcloth.'
> ...They have the power to shut the sky, that no rain may fall during the days of their prophesying [possibly Elijah], and they have power over the waters to turn them into blood and to strike the earth with every kind of plague, as often as they desire [possibly Moses, or Enoch along with Elijah never died]. And when they have finished their testimony, the beast that rises from the bottomless pit will make war on them and conquer them and kill them, and their dead bodies

220 Luke 1:17
221 John 1:21
222 Luke 1:17
223 2 Kings 1:8; Matthew 3:4
224 Matthew 3:1; 1 Kings 17:1, 19:4
225 1 Kings 18:17; Matthew 14:3

will lie in the street of the great city that symbolically
is called Sodom and Egypt, where their Lord was
crucified. For three and a half days some from the
peoples and tribes and languages and nations will
gaze at their dead bodies and refuse to let them be
placed in a tomb, and those who dwell on the earth
will rejoice over them and make merry and exchange
presents, because these two prophets had been a
torment to those who dwell on the earth. But after the
three and a half days a breath of life from God entered
them, and they stood up on their feet, and great fear
fell on those who saw them. Then they heard a loud
voice from heaven saying to them, 'Come up here!'
And they went up to heaven in a cloud, and their
enemies watched them. And at that hour there was
a great earthquake, and a tenth of the city fell. Seven
thousand people were killed in the earthquake, and
the rest were terrified and gave glory to the God
of heaven."

It is common among Bible scholars to identify one of these witnesses as Elijah. The prophecy is that of a prophet who would shut the sky and prevent rain from falling, which corresponds exactly with Elijah. It makes sense that Elijah, one of God's toughest prophetic soldiers, would be spared death and sent back for the last battle on earth before the Second Coming of Jesus. We are told that both prophetic witnesses will be killed and will be the risen from death to vindicate his loyalty to the Lord. The second prophetic witness is believed by some to be either Enoch or Moses. Since Enoch did not die,[226] these are the only two men who escaped death, which leads some to conclude that their death would come in the last days. Others

---

226 Genesis 5:14

believe that the second witness is Moses because the ability to turn the waters to blood echoes the Exodus 7:14-25 account where Moses struck his staff in the Nile, and it turned to blood. One day, we will know for sure.

Jesus' Second Coming

Until that day, as we see Elijah ascending into Heaven, we are to remember that it was a foreshadowing of the Lord Jesus' ascension after His rise from death to forgive sin. Acts 1:9-11 reports:

> *"...he was lifted up, and a cloud took him out of their sight. And while they were gazing into heaven as he went, behold, two men stood by them in white robes, and said, 'Men of Galilee, why do you stand looking into heaven? This Jesus, who was taken up from you into heaven, will come in the same way as you saw him go into heaven.'"*

One day, perhaps soon, the Lord Jesus, who went up, will come down one last time to battle evil kings in the mold of Ahab on yet another mountain, just like Elijah. Zechariah 14:3-5,9 says of Jesus' Second Coming, "Then the Lord will go out and fight against those nations as when he fights on a day of battle. On that day his feet shall stand on the Mount of Olives that lies before Jerusalem on the east, and the Mount of Olives shall be split in two from east to west by a very wide valley, so that one half of the Mount shall move northward, and the other half southward...Then the Lord my God will come, and all the holy ones with him...And the Lord will be king over all the earth. On that day the Lord will be one and his name one."

Other Scriptures give additional details about Jesus' Second Coming. Philippians 3:20-21 says:

"...our citizenship is in heaven, and from it we await a Savior, the Lord Jesus Christ, who will transform our lowly body to be like his glorious body, by the power that enables him even to subject all things to himself."

Matthew 24:27 says:

"For as the lightning comes from the east and shines as far as the west, so will be the coming of the Son of Man."

Matthew 24:30–31 says:

"Then will appear in heaven the sign of the Son of Man, and then all the tribes of the earth will mourn, and they will see the Son of Man coming on the clouds of heaven with power and great glory. And he will send out his angels with a loud trumpet call, and they will gather his elect from the four winds, from one end of heaven to the other."

Matthew 25:31–32 says:

"When the Son of Man comes in his glory, and all the angels with him, then he will sit on his glorious throne. Before him will be gathered all the nations, and he will separate people one from another as a shepherd separates the sheep from the goats." Mark 13:32 says of when Jesus will return, "But concerning that day or that hour, no one knows, not even the angels in heaven, nor the Son, but only the Father." All we know in the Bible is that there will one day be the "day of the Lord", and so we should live every day ready for His Coming.

Some theologians have referred to the Second and Final Coming of King Jesus as the Parousia, "*Parousía* was in use as a technical term for the arrival of the emperor or other dignitary when he visited his subjects...This was a great event, sometimes marked by the striking of special coins or the erection of monuments. The word thus has overtones of greatness that should be kept in mind when it is used of Christ's return."[br]

On the day of Jesus' Second Coming following the crucifixion and resurrection of Elijah, all believers will experience the same kind of homecoming that he did when God took him up in the clouds. To encourage us about believers who have died (asleep) and our own death, 1 Thessalonians 4:13-18 says:

> *"...we do not want you to be uninformed, brothers, about those who are asleep, that you may not grieve as others do who have no hope. For since we believe that Jesus died and rose again, even so, through Jesus, God will bring with him those who have fallen asleep. For this we declare to you by a word from the Lord, that we who are alive, who are left until the coming of the Lord, will not precede those who have fallen asleep. For the Lord himself will descend from heaven with a cry of command, with the voice of an archangel, and with the sound of the trumpet of God. And the dead in Christ will rise first. Then we who are alive, who are left, will be caught up together with them in the clouds to meet the Lord in the air, and so we will always be with the Lord. Therefore encourage one another with these words."*

Be encouraged. Your chariot is coming, and you will be riding off into the sunset. Until then, repent of sin, be filled with the Holy Spirit of Elijah, and publicly take your stand for your Lord despite the battles that will come from the old demons working in new days.

Appendix A:
Elijah Outside 1-2 Kings

Elijah is listed along with Moses as one of the most towering prophets in the Bible. In addition to his appearances in 1 Kings 17-2 Kings 2, which are the focus of this Bible study, he also appears on numerous occasions throughout the rest of Scripture.

A Bible dictionary says, "Elijah is the fourth most frequently cited OT figure in the NT (Moses, eighty times; Abraham, seventy-three times; David, fifty-nine times; Elijah, twenty-nine times). All but two of these references are in the Gospels (Rom 11:2; Jas 5:17). Only two of these citations are in John (1:21, 25). The remaining twenty-five references within the Synoptics are widely distributed, though most appear in at least two of the Synoptics. One text is unique to Matthew (11:14). Two are unique to Luke (1:17; 4:25–26). Some passages are shared by all of the Synoptics (Mt 16:14…Mk 8:28 and Lk 9:19; Mt 17:3–4, 10–12…Mk 9:4–5, 11–13 and Lk 9:30, 33). Some material is shared by Mark and Matthew (Mk 15:35–36…Mt 27:47, 49) and one passage by Mark and Luke (Mk 6:15…Lk 9:8). Allusions to Malachi also appear (Mk 1:2–3; Mt 10:11; Lk 7:27), as do references to a ministry of fire (Mt 3:11; Lk 9:54; 12:49), recalling Elijah's ministry of judgment at Mt. Carmel (1 Kings 18) and his calling fire down on the messengers of King Ahaziah (2 Kings 1)."[bs]

Elijah is also intimated numerous times.[227] However, for the sake of this Bible study, we will simply list the most prominent mentions of Elijah in the Scriptures. We will start with the Old Testament, and then examine the New Testament.

Elijah in the Old Testament

→ **2 Chronicles 21:12–15**—And a letter came to him from Elijah the prophet, saying, "Thus says the Lord, the God of David your father, 'Because you have not walked in the ways of Jehoshaphat your father, or in the ways of Asa king of Judah, but have walked in the way of the kings of Israel and have enticed Judah and the inhabitants of Jerusalem into whoredom, as the house of Ahab led Israel into whoredom, and also you have killed your brothers, of your father's house, who were better than you, behold, the Lord will bring a great plague on your people, your children, your wives, and all your possessions, and you yourself will have a severe sickness with a disease of your bowels, until your bowels come out because of the disease, day by day.'"

→ **Malachi 4:4–6**—"Remember the law of my servant Moses, the statutes and rules that I commanded him at Horeb for all Israel. 'Behold, I will send you Elijah the prophet before the great and awesome day of the Lord comes. And he will turn the hearts of fathers to their children and the hearts of children to their fathers, lest I come and strike the land with a decree of utter destruction.'"

---

227 e.g., Luke 4:25-27, 7:16, 9:8, 9:19, 9:62

Elijah in the New Testament

→ Matthew 11:11–15 — Truly, I say to you, among those born of women there has arisen no one greater than John the Baptist. Yet the one who is least in the kingdom of heaven is greater than he. From the days of John the Baptist until now the kingdom of heaven has suffered violence, and the violent take it by force. For all the Prophets and the Law prophesied until John, and if you are willing to accept it, he is Elijah who is to come. He who has ears to hear, let him hear.

→ Matthew 16:13–15 (also in Mark 8:27-30; Luke 9:18-20) — Now when Jesus came into the district of Caesarea Philippi, he asked his disciples, "Who do people say that the Son of Man is?" And they said, "Some say John the Baptist, others say Elijah, and others Jeremiah or one of the prophets." He said to them, "But who do you say that I am?"

→ Matthew 17:1–13 (also in Mark 9:2-13; Luke 9:28-36) — And after six days Jesus took with him Peter and James, and John his brother, and led them up a high mountain by themselves. And he was transfigured before them, and his face shone like the sun, and his clothes became white as light. And behold, there appeared to them Moses and Elijah, talking with him. And Peter said to Jesus, "Lord, it is good that we are here. If you wish, I will make three tents here, one for you and one for Moses and one for Elijah." He was still speaking when, behold, a bright cloud overshadowed them, and a voice from the cloud said, "This is my beloved Son, with whom I am well pleased; listen to him." When the disciples heard this, they fell on their faces and were terrified. But Jesus came and touched them, saying, "Rise, and have no fear." And when they lifted up their eyes, they saw no one but Jesus only. And as they were coming down the mountain, Jesus commanded them, "Tell no one the vision, until the Son of Man is raised from the dead." And the disciples asked him, "Then why do the scribes say that first Elijah must come?" He answered, "Elijah does come, and he will restore all things. But I tell you that Elijah has already come, and they did not recognize him, but did to him whatever they pleased. So also the Son of Man will certainly suffer at their hands." Then the disciples understood that he was speaking to them of John the Baptist.

→ **Matthew 27:46–50 (also in Mark 15:34-36)** — And about the ninth hour Jesus cried out with a loud voice, saying, "Eli, Eli, lema sabachthani?" that is, "My God, my God, why have you forsaken me?" And some of the bystanders, hearing it, said, "This man is calling Elijah." And one of them at once ran and took a sponge, filled it with sour wine, and put it on a reed and gave it to him to drink. But the others said, "Wait, let us see whether Elijah will come to save him." And Jesus cried out again with a loud voice and yielded up his spirit.

→ **Mark 6:14–16 (also in Luke 9:7-9)** — King Herod heard of it, for Jesus' name had become known. Some said, "John the Baptist has been raised from the dead. That is why these miraculous powers are at work in him." But others said, "He is Elijah." And others said, "He is a prophet, like one of the prophets of old." But when Herod heard of it, he said, "John, whom I beheaded, has been raised."

→ **Luke 1:16–17** — "...And he [John the Baptizer] will turn many of the children of Israel to the Lord their God, and he will go before him in the spirit and power of Elijah, to turn the hearts of the fathers to the children, and the disobedient to the wisdom of the just, to make ready for the Lord a people prepared."

→ **Luke 4:24–26**—And he said, "Truly, I say to you, no prophet is acceptable in his hometown. But in truth, I tell you, there were many widows in Israel in the days of Elijah, when the heavens were shut up three years and six months, and a great famine came over all the land, and Elijah was sent to none of them but only to Zarephath, in the land of Sidon, to a woman who was a widow..."

→ **John 1:19–23**—And this is the testimony of John, when the Jews sent priests and Levites from Jerusalem to ask him, "Who are you?" He confessed, and did not deny, but confessed, "I am not the Christ." And they asked him, "What then? Are you Elijah?" He said, "I am not." "Are you the Prophet?" And he answered, "No." So they said to him, "Who are you? We need to give an answer to those who sent us. What do you say about yourself?" He said, "I am the voice of one crying out in the wilderness, 'Make straight the way of the Lord,' as the prophet Isaiah said."

→ **Romans 11:1–6**—I ask, then, has God rejected his people? By no means! For I myself am an Israelite, a descendant of Abraham, a member of the tribe of Benjamin. God has not rejected his people whom he foreknew. Do you not know what the Scripture says of Elijah, how he appeals to God against Israel? "Lord, they have killed your prophets, they have demolished your altars, and I alone am left, and they seek my life." But what is God's reply to him? "I have kept for myself seven thousand men who have not bowed the knee to Baal." So too at the present time there is a remnant, chosen by grace. But if it is by grace, it is no longer on the basis of works; otherwise grace would no longer be grace.

→ **James 5:17–18**—Elijah was a man with a nature like ours, and he prayed fervently that it might not rain, and for three years and six months it did not rain on the earth. Then he prayed again, and heaven gave rain, and the earth bore its fruit.

→ Revelation 11:3,6–13—"...I will grant authority to my two witnesses, and they will prophesy for 1,260 days, clothed in sackcloth"...They have the power to shut the sky, that no rain may fall during the days of their prophesying [possibly Elijah], and they have power over the waters to turn them into blood and to strike the earth with every kind of plague, as often as they desire [possibly Moses, or Enoch along with Elijah never died]. And when they have finished their testimony, the beast that rises from the bottomless pit will make war on them and conquer them and kill them, and their dead bodies will lie in the street of the great city that symbolically is called Sodom and Egypt, where their Lord was crucified. For three and a half days some from the peoples and tribes and languages and nations will gaze at their dead bodies and refuse to let them be placed in a tomb, and those who dwell on the earth will rejoice over them and make merry and exchange presents, because these two prophets had been a torment to those who dwell on the earth. But after the three and a half days a breath of life from God entered them, and they stood up on their feet, and great fear fell on those who saw them. Then they heard a loud voice from heaven saying to them, "Come up here!" And they went up to heaven in a cloud, and their enemies watched them. And at that hour there was a great earthquake, and a tenth of the city fell. Seven thousand people were killed in the earthquake, and the rest were terrified and gave glory to the God of heaven.

Appendix B:
Can a Christian be Demon Possessed?

In our study of Elijah, a lot has been said about demonic beings and their interaction with human beings. This will likely cause some people to ask what degree of influence can a demonic being have in the life of a Christian? Commonly, the question is posed as, "Can a Christian be demon possessed?"

This is a very important question that is a bit complicated. Because demonic beings are unseen (unless they choose to manifest in a physical form), understanding their involvement in our life is more difficult than discerning the degree to which a human being has influence in our life.

In *Win Your War*, my wife Grace and I delve much deeper into this and other issues regarding the demonic realm. What follows is a summary of what we expand on in that book.

Non-Christians and Demons

For the non-Christian, it is possible to give oneself over to sin, rebellion, and evil to the extent that an unclean spirit takes up residence in and ownership over someone. The Bible often refers to our sinful flesh as being a doorway to the demonic through sinful living. The New Testament Gospels are filled with reports about Jesus' ministry of deliverance. Curiously, Jesus is the first person in the Bible to cast a demon out of someone; the Old

Testament has no record of this ever happening prior to Jesus' ministry. However, all demonic deliverance accounts in the New Testament follow Jesus' pattern. Here are a few examples from just one New Testament book.

→ **Matthew 4:24**—So his [Jesus'] fame spread throughout all Syria, and they brought him all the sick, those afflicted with various diseases and pains, those oppressed by demons, those having seizures, and paralytics, and he healed them.

→ **Matthew 8:16**—That evening they brought to him many who were oppressed by demons, and he cast out the spirits with a word and healed all who were sick.

→ **Matthew 9:32–33**—As they were going away, behold, a demon-oppressed man who was mute was brought to him. And when the demon had been cast out, the mute man spoke. And the crowds marveled, saying, "Never was anything like this seen in Israel."

→ **Matthew 12:22**—Then a demon-oppressed man who was blind and mute was brought to him, and he healed him, so that the man spoke and saw.

→ **Matthew 15:22, 28**—And behold, a Canaanite woman from that region came out and was crying, "Have mercy on me, O Lord, Son of David; my daughter is severely oppressed by a demon."…Then Jesus answered her, "O woman, great is your faith! Be it done for you as you desire." And her daughter was healed instantly.

→ **Matthew 17:18**—And Jesus rebuked the demon, and it came out of him, and the boy was healed instantly.

The Bible is very clear. Demonic spirits can overcome some non-Christians to the point that they suffer mental and physical anguish. Not all mental and physical anguish is the result of demonic control, but some of it is. In such circumstances, a doctor to serve the body, a counselor to serve the mind, and the power of God to deliver the soul can all be helpful to minister to the whole person.

Christians and Demons

How about a Christian? Can a Christian be demon possessed? On this issue, as they say, the devil is in the details. *Oxford English Dictionary* gives the following as the first three definitions of the word possess:

1. **Have as belonging to one; own.**

2. **Have possession of as distinct from ownership.**

3. **Have as an ability, quality, or characteristic.**[bt]

Definition #1

In the first sense, a Christian cannot belong to Satan; he cannot own us. The transfer of ownership for people is always and only one way—people who belonged to Satan and darkness become God's people in the light. "He has delivered us from the domain of darkness and transferred us to the kingdom of his beloved Son."[228] Salvation is a miracle of God where we "turn from darkness to light and from the power of Satan to God."[229]

Some people ask if a Christian can lose their salvation, which is the wrong question. Salvation does not belong to us, but rather "Salvation belongs to the Lord!"[230] Therefore, the

228 Colossians 1:13

229 Acts 26:18

230 Jonah 2:9

question is, Can God lose a Christian? The answer to that is no. With total confidence, the Holy Spirit says through Paul, "I am sure that neither...angels nor rulers...nor powers, nor height nor depth, nor anything else in all creation, will be able to separate us from the love of God in Christ Jesus our Lord."[231] This is because a Christian is forever "sealed" with the Holy Spirit as the "guarantee" of eternal life.[232]

We have five children. We both love babies. When the kids were little and entirely dependent upon us, we would often snuggle up as a couple with them. The safest place for our children was in our arms. Jesus uses this kind of word picture, saying, "I give them eternal life, and they will never perish, and no one will snatch them out of my hand. My Father, who has given them to me, is greater than all, and no one is able to snatch them out of the Father's hand."[233]

Definition #2

In the second sense of the word possess, a Christian can be internally influenced by the demonic without ownership of their soul transferring to the devil. Think of your life like your home since you live in both. You are the legal resident of your home, and no one else has the right to move in unless you give them permission. Now, let's say that some bad people come to your house, you open the door to welcome them in, and they decide to stay and make your life miserable. They possess no legal right to be there, but they are willing to squat until you exercise your legal authority and demand that they vacate your home. On rare occasions through habitual sin, deep unbelief, dark addiction,

231 Romans 8:38–39
232 Ephesians 1:13–14
233 John 10:28–29

or occult activity, a Christian can open the door to internal demonic influence that does not have any legal authority and can be evicted in Jesus' name. This may include habitual living in the flesh, or the continuation of generational sin that has had a foothold for so long in a family that it has become a stronghold.

In Acts 5:1–11 we meet "Ananias, with his wife Sapphira." After watching Barnabas sell land and give the proceeds to the church, they decided to do the same. They sold a piece of property, but rather than tithing the entire amount they had promised to the Lord, with the wife's consent, the husband "kept back for himself some of the proceeds and brought only a part of it and laid it at the apostles' feet" (v. 2). These church members were guilty of lying to the Lord and their leaders while stealing. Peter asked, "Ananias, why has Satan led your heart to lie to the Holy Spirit?" (v. 3) Then he told the couple: "You have not lied to man but to God" (v. 4). Internally influenced by Satan, both the husband and wife died right there on the spot, causing awe and fear among the other Christians.

Because Satan internally influenced them, some speculate that these two were not, in fact, Christians. Here is what one New Testament commentary says:

"Were Ananias and Sapphira really believers? Scholars answer in at least two ways: 1) they were members of the church (so-called nominal Christians) who never entered in faith into a personal saving relationship with Jesus; 2) they were Christians whose sin (possibly the sin unto death of 1 John 5:16–17; cf. 1 Cor. 11:27–30) God punished as an example to the church but who gained eternal salvation. The entire narrative seems to indicate that these people were born-again Christians and very much a part of the Jerusalem congregation. It is not unusual in the Scripture to send death coming to believers at the hand of God."[bu]

Christians can open themselves up to the internal influence of demonic powers through participating in evil, even though they still belong to God as His possession. Some argue that God and Satan cannot occupy the same space, but that is possible if the Lord permits it. As one example, in Job 1, Satan clearly comes into God's presence, and they have a conversation regarding Job.

Definition #3

In the third sense of the word possess, it is possible for a Christian to manifest demonic character or say things with demonic origins. As Jesus was teaching about His death, "Peter took him aside and began to rebuke him, saying, 'Far be it from you, Lord! is shall never happen to you.'" In response Jesus "turned and said to Peter, 'Get behind me, Satan!'"[234] Peter was a believer, but in that instance, he echoed what Satan was saying and rebuked the Lord as if Jesus were sinning. Jesus identified Satan as the ultimate origin of what Peter was doing and saying.

In summary, a Christian can be lied to, tempted by, and attacked from Satan just as Jesus Christ was. However, it is impossible for a demon to own a believer as its possession. While God cannot lose a Christian, a person can fake having faith. This was precisely the case with Judas Iscariot. He was incredibly covert, hiding the fact that, for years as Jesus' bookkeeper, "he was a thief, and having charge of the moneybag he used to help himself to what was put into it."[235] Even though Judas outwardly looked like a believer, he was not. Knowing that many would wrongly assume Judas was a believer whom

---

234 Matthew 16:21-23

235 John 12:6

"Satan entered,"[236] Jesus made it clear that Judas was never a real Christian. Jesus said of His disciples minus Judas, "I protected them and kept them safe…None has been lost except the one doomed to destruction."[237]

For the real Christian, there is no excuse for permitting internal influence by demonic forces. The problem is not out there in demons but ultimately in us. We cannot control what demons do, but we can control what we do since "each person is tempted when he is lured and enticed by his own desire."[238] Demons cannot control believers or make us do anything because we have the weapons to win our spiritual wars. There is always a way to escape a demonic attack.[239]

Becoming a Christian is both receiving Jesus and rejecting Satan. On the Old Testament Day of Atonement, two animals were sacrificed for this very reason. The first animal was a spotless lamb that died as a substitute for the sinner, showing the receiving of Jesus. The second animal was a scapegoat to which sin was reckoned as it was driven away, showing the renouncing of Satan. Heiser adds this interesting detail in his book *The Unseen Realm*: "The wilderness was where Israelites believed 'desert demons,' including Azazel, lived. The Azazel material is especially telling, since…[the] Jewish practice of the Day of Atonement ritual in Jesus' day included driving the goat 'for Azazel' into the desert outside Jerusalem and pushing it over a cliff so it could not return. The wilderness was a place associated with the demonic, so it's no surprise that this is where Jesus meets the devil."[bv]

Similarly, the baptismal formula of the early church included both receiving Jesus and renouncing Satan: "The

---

236 Luke 22:3

237 John 17:12

238 James 1:14

239 1 Corinthians 10:13

renunciation of the devil at baptism is a custom which goes back certainly to the 2nd century."[bw] We further learn, "The first witness for renunciations...is Tertullian...When entering the water, we make profession of the Christian faith in the words of its rule, we bear public testimony that we have renounced the devil, his pomp, and his angels."[bx]

The key to living free from demonic influence as a Christian is twofold. One, you must receive Jesus Christ and His defeat of the demonic. Two, you must renounce any ground you give to the demonic through such things as sin, rebellion, unbelief, pride, and the other matters we discuss throughout this book. This is precisely what James 4:7 means when it says, "Submit yourselves therefore to God [receive]. Resist the devil [renounce], and he will flee from you" (amplification added).

In his book *Deeper Walk*, Marcus Warner offers a helpful prayer pattern for anyone who wants to remove demonic activity in their life:

1. **Confess**—in prayer, confess and repent of anything that would provide a demonic foothold in your life (habitual sin, believing lies, inner vows, occultic activity, sexual rebellion, trauma, bitterness, ungodly relationships, etc.)

2. **Cancel**—in spiritual warfare, through our sin we retreat and give ground to our enemy. In prayer, we cancel the ground we have given in any area of our life (e.g., thoughts we think in our mind, things we consume in our body, images we consume with our eyes, relationships that encourage us to sin against God). You should then invite the Holy Spirit to fill any and every area where you have given ground to the Enemy.

3. **Command**—using your authority in Christ, in prayer you can command any demons, including their works and

effects (sometimes this is what causes physical sickness and torment) to leave you and every area of your life in Jesus' name.

4. **Commit**—in prayer, you commit yourself to living in the Spirit, seeking to obey God as a surrendered worshipper in every area of your life.

For the non-Christian, they do not have the Holy Spirit or the authority that Christ shares with His people. The first thing a non-Christian needs is to repent of their sin and receive Jesus Christ as their Lord and Savior.

Once someone is a Christian, they do not have to tolerate evil or the demonic and can prayerfully invite the Holy Spirit to deliver them from evil and fill them. This is a healthy habit for your soul that too few Christians practice as they know far more about how to keep their body healthy than their soul. God loves you and wants the best for you, so please enjoy the fullness of freedom in Christ!

About Pastor Mark
& RealFaith Ministries

With Pastor Mark, it's all about Jesus! He is a spiritual leader, prolific author, and compelling speaker, but at his core, he is a family man. Mark and his wife Grace have been married and doing vocational ministry together since 1993 and, along with their five kids, planted Trinity Church in Scottsdale, Arizona as a family ministry.

Pastor Mark, Grace, and their oldest daughter, Ashley, also started RealFaith Ministries, which contains a mountain of Bible teaching for men, women, couples, parents, pastors, leaders, Spanish speakers, and more, which you can access by visiting **RealFaith.com** or downloading the **RealFaith app**.

With a master's degree in exegetical theology from Western Seminary in Portland, Oregon, he has spent the better part of his life teaching verse-by-verse through books of the Bible, contextualizing its timeless truths and never shying away from challenging, convicting passages that speak to the heart of current cultural dilemmas.

Together, Mark and Grace have co-authored *Win Your War*, *Real Marriage*, and *Real Romance: Sex in the Song of Songs*, and he co-authored a father-daughter project called *Pray Like Jesus* with his daughter, Ashley. Pastor Mark has also written numerous other books including *Spirit-Filled Jesus*, *Who Do You Think You Are?*, *Vintage Jesus*, and *Doctrine*.

If you have any prayer requests for us, questions for future Ask Pastor Mark or Dear Grace videos, or a testimony regarding how God has used this and other resources to help you learn God's word, we would love to hear from you at **hello@realfaith.com**.

Endnotes

a https://www.nationalgeographic.com/travel/article/where-to-go-to-explore-pagan-culture

b This connection appears in Jonathan Cahn's book *The Return of the Gods*.

c https://www.cdc.gov/mmwr/volumes/72/su/su7201a1.htm

d https://www.newsweek.com/satan-getting-hot-hell-american-pop-culture-1790669

e Michael S. Heiser, *Angels: What the Bible Really Says about God's Heavenly Host* (Bellingham, WA: Lexham Press, 2018), 12.

f Derek R. Brown and E. Tod Twist, *Romans*, ed. Douglas Mangum, Lexham Research Commentaries (Bellingham, WA: Lexham Press, 2014), Ro 11:1–10.

g Ronald D. Roberts, "Miracle," ed. John D. Barry et al., *The Lexham Bible Dictionary* (Bellingham, WA: Lexham Press, 2016)

h William Arndt et al., *A Greek-English Lexicon of the New Testament and Other Early Christian Literature* (Chicago: University of Chicago Press, 2000), 549.

i   James R. Adair Jr., "Man of God," ed. David Noel Freedman, Allen C. Myers, and Astrid B. Beck, *Eerdmans Dictionary of the Bible* (Grand Rapids, MI: W.B. Eerdmans, 2000), 854.

j   Francis Brown, Samuel Rolles Driver, and Charles Augustus Briggs, *Enhanced Brown-Driver-Briggs Hebrew and English Lexicon* (Oxford: Clarendon Press, 1977), 747–748.

k   Clinton E. Arnold, "Syncretism," ed. Ralph P. Martin and Peter H. Davids, *Dictionary of the Later New Testament and Its Developments* (Downers Grove, IL: InterVarsity Press, 1997), 1146.

l   Ian W. K. Koiter, "Apostasy," ed. John D. Barry et al., *The Lexham Bible Dictionary* (Bellingham, WA: Lexham Press, 2016).

m   Willem VanGemeren, ed., *New International Dictionary of Old Testament Theology and Exegesis* (Grand Rapids, MI: Zondervan Publishing House, 1997), 941.

n   Clinton E. Arnold, *Powers of Darkness: Principalities and Powers in Paul's Letters* (Downers Grove, IL: InterVarsity, 1992), 67.

o   https://www.nationalreview.com/news/disney-executive-producer-admits-to-gay-agenda-adding-queerness-wherever-she-could/

p   https://www.snopes.com/fact-check/little-demon-disney-show/

q   Pauline A. Viviano, "Ethbaal (Person)," ed. David Noel Freedman, *The Anchor Yale Bible Dictionary* (New York: Doubleday, 1992), 645.

r   Charles Fox Burney, "ETHBAAL," ed. James Hastings et al., *A Dictionary of the Bible: Dealing with Its Language, Literature, and Contents Including the Biblical Theology* (New York; Edinburgh: Charles Scribner's Sons; T. & T. Clark, 1911–1912), 777.

s   John A. Selbie, "JEZEBEL," ed. James Hastings et al., *A Dictionary of the Bible: Dealing with Its Language, Literature, and Contents Including the Biblical Theology* (New York; Edinburgh: Charles Scribner's Sons; T. & T. Clark, 1911–1912), 656.

t   Chad Brand et al., eds., "Jezebel," *Holman Illustrated Bible Dictionary* (Nashville, TN: Holman Bible Publishers, 2003), 921.

u   https://blacklivesmatter.com/about

v   Ibid.

w   https://www.adweek.com/performance-marketing/why-lgbtq-pride-festivals-becoming-black-lives-matter-protests/

x   Excerpt From: Religion and Female Body in Ancient Judaism and Its Environments Géza G. Xeravits. https://itunes.apple.com/WebObjects/MZStore.woa/wa/viewBook?id=0

y   F. L. Cross and Elizabeth A. Livingstone, eds., *The Oxford Dictionary of the Christian Church* (Oxford; New York: Oxford University Press, 2005), 116.

z   Winfried Corduan, "Baal," ed. John D. Barry et al., *The Lexham Bible Dictionary* (Bellingham, WA: Lexham Press, 2016).

aa   William L. Kelly, "Elijah Cycle," ed. John D. Barry et al., *The Lexham Bible Dictionary* (Bellingham, WA: Lexham Press, 2016).

ab   https://www.un.org/en/observances/earth-day

ac   Robert B. Hughes and J. Carl Laney, *Tyndale Concise Bible Commentary*, The Tyndale Reference Library (Wheaton, IL: Tyndale House Publishers, 2001), 136.

ad   Leland Ryken, James C. Wilhoit, et al., eds., *Dictionary of Biblical Imagery* (Downers Grove, IL: InterVarsity, 1998), s.v. "Humor," 762.

ae   Charles Haddon Spurgeon, "The Uses of Anecdotes and Illustrations," in *Lectures to My Students* (Grand Rapids, MI: Zondervan, 1954), 389.

af   https://www.webmd.com/sex/what-is-furry-sex

ag   Eckhardt, *Deliverance and Spiritual Warfare Manual*, 208.

ah   Eckhardt, *Deliverance and Spiritual Warfare Manual*, 227–28.

ai   Eckhardt, *Deliverance and Spiritual Warfare Manual*, 208.

aj   https://dictionary.apa.org/codependency

ak John Eckhardt, *Deliverance and Spiritual Warfare Manual* (Lake Mary, FL: Charisma House, 2014), 237.

al John Eckhardt, *Deliverance and Spiritual Warfare Manual* (Lake Mary, FL: Charisma House, 2014), 30.

am R. K. Harrison, *Evangelical Dictionary of Biblical Theology*, Baker Reference Library, ed. Walter A. Elwell (Grand Rapids, MI: Baker Book House, 1996), 21.

an Leland Ryken, James C. Wilhoit, and Tremper Longman III, eds., *Dictionary of Biblical Imagery* (Downers Grove, IL: InterVarsity Press, 2000), s.v. "Angels," 23.

ao https://www.ncbi.nlm.nih.gov/pmc/articles/PMC3535560/

ap https://www.youtube.com/watch?v=I8BRdwgPChQ

aq David Mark Rathel, "Eunuch," ed. John D. Barry et al., *The Lexham Bible Dictionary* (Bellingham, WA: Lexham Press, 2016).

ar R. Alan Cole, *Galatians: An Introduction and Commentary*, vol. 9, Tyndale New Testament Commentaries (Downers Grove, IL: InterVarsity Press, 1989), 130.

as Ronald Y. K. Fung, *The Epistle to the Galatians*, The New International Commentary on the New Testament (Grand Rapids, MI: Wm. B. Eerdmans Publishing Co., 1988), 242.

at https://www.english-heritage.org.uk/learn/histories/lgbtq-history/the-galli/#:~:text=The%20Galli%20were%20priests%20in,dressed%20exclusively%20in%20women's%20clothing

au https://rainbowmessenger.blog/2022/04/04/the-trans-god/

av https://juicyecumenism.com/2022/10/07/methodist-drag-queen-ms-penny-cost-returns-in-florida-childrens-sermon/

aw Will Roscoe, "Priests of the Goddess: Gender Transgression in Ancient Religion," *History of Religions* 35:3 (1996):195-196.

ax Ibid.

ay Will Roscoe, "Priests of the Goddess: Gender Transgression in Ancient Religion," *History of Religions* 35:3 (1996):197.

az Michael S. Heiser, *The Unseen Realm: Recovering the Supernatural Worldview of the Bible* (Bellingham, WA: Lexham Press, 2015), 121-22.

ba Will Roscoe, "Priests of the Goddess: Gender Transgression in Ancient Religion," *History of Religions* 35:3 (1996):201-202.

bb Will Roscoe, "Priests of the Goddess: Gender Transgression in Ancient Religion," *History of Religions* 35:3 (1996):217

bc Will Roscoe, "Priests of the Goddess: Gender Transgression in Ancient Religion," *History of Religions* 35:3 (1996):205-206

bd Excerpt From: Religion and Female Body in Ancient Judaism and Its Environments Géza G. Xeravits. https://itunes.apple.com/WebObjects/MZStore.woa/wa/viewBook?id=0 "Translated by Clarence Forbes, (FORBES, Firmicus Maternus, 50–51). For a more detailed analysis of the quoted passage, and about the origin, history and peculiarities of the institution of the galli, examined as a representative example of ritual gender transgression see ROSCOE, Priests of the Goddess, esp. 195–202."

be St. Augustine, De civitate Dei, 7.26

bf Warren W. Wiersbe, *Wiersbe's Expository Outlines on the Old Testament* (Wheaton, IL: Victor Books, 1993), 1 Ki 18.

bg https://www.etymonline.com/word/passive#:~:text=passive%20(adj.),undergoing%20hardship%22%20(14c.)

bh https://www.reuters.com/world/us/stormy-daniels-woman-center-trump-indictment-is-porn-star-turned-ghostbuster-2023-03-31/

bi https://nymag.com/press/2023/04/on-the-cover-stormy-daniels-profiled-by-olivia-nuzzi.html

bj https://www.foxnews.com/media/stormy-daniels-summon-spirits-magic-cards-eyes-filled-tears

bk https://thespectator.com/book-and-art/stormy-daniels-good-fortune-tarot-reading/

bl https://religionnews.com/2022/02/28/stormy-daniels-donald-trump-michael-avenatti-defend-herself-at-lawyers-trial/

bm https://nymag.com/intelligencer/article/stormy-daniels-donald-trump-arrest.html

bn Daniel I. Morrison, "Antichrist," ed. John D. Barry et al., *The Lexham Bible Dictionary* (Bellingham, WA: Lexham Press, 2016).

bo S. B. Noegel, "Phoenicia, Phoenicians," ed. Bill T. Arnold and H. G. M. Williamson, *Dictionary of the Old Testament: Historical Books* (Downers Grove, IL: InterVarsity Press, 2005), 797.

bp The concept of the assertive personality and lots of other helpful insights can be found in Steve Sampson's books "Confronting Jezebel" and "Discerning and Defeating the Ahab Spirit."

bq Walter A. Elwell and Barry J. Beitzel, "Type, Typology," *Baker Encyclopedia of the Bible* (Grand Rapids, MI: Baker Book House, 1988), 2109–2110.

br L. Morris, "Parousia," ed. Geoffrey W. Bromiley, *The International Standard Bible Encyclopedia*, Revised (Wm. B. Eerdmans, 1979–1988), 664.

bs D. L. Bock, "Elijah and Elisha," ed. Joel B. Green and Scot McKnight, *Dictionary of Jesus and the Gospels* (Downers Grove, IL: InterVarsity Press, 1992), 204.

bt Oxford Living Dictionaries, s.v. "possess," accessed June 5, 2019, https://en.oxforddictionaries.com/definition/possess.

bu Kenneth O. Gangel, *Holman New Testament Commentary: Acts* (Nashville: Broadman & Holman, 1998), 82.

bv Heiser, The Unseen Realm, 277.

bw A. J. Maclean, "Abrenuntio," in Encyclopædia of Religion and Ethics, vol. 1, eds. James Hastings, John A. Selbie, and Louis H. Gray (New York: Charles Scribner's Sons, 1910), 38.

bx Maclean, Encyclopædia of Religion and Ethics, 39.

Made in United States
Troutdale, OR
06/01/2025